Desk Reference to the

Diagnostic Criteria

from

DSM-III

The correct citation for this book is:
American Psychiatric Association;
Desk Reference to the
Diagnostic Criteria from
Diagnostic and Statistical Manual of
Mental Disorders, Third Edition,
Washington, D.C., APA, 1982.

ISBN 0–89042–046–7

First printing, September 1982

Table of Contents

Introduction

One of the most important features of DSM-III is the provision of diagnostic criteria to improve the reliability of diagnostic judgments. With this approach, the clinician's task is twofold: to determine the presence or absence of specific clinical features, and then to use the criteria as guidelines for making the diagnosis Another important feature of DSM-III is the inclusion of decision trees to aid the clinician in understanding the organization and hierarchical structure of the classification. The clinician may wish to have available a small booklet to be used as a quick reference that contains only the classification, the diagnostic criteria, a listing of the most important conditions to be considered in the differential diagnosis, and the decision trees.

Proper use of this booklet requires familiarity with the description of the diagnostic categories and the glossary of definitions of technical terms contained in DSM-III.

Robert L. Spitzer, M.D.
Chairperson,
Task Force on
Nomenclature and Statistics

Use of The Desk Reference

MULTIAXIAL EVALUATION

A multiaxial evaluation requires that every case be assessed on each of several "axes," each of which refers to a different class of information. In order for the system to have maximal clinical usefulness, there must be a limited number of axes; there are five in the DSM-III multiaxial classification. The first three axes constitute the official diagnostic assessment.

Each individual is evaluated on each of these axes:

Axis I Clinical Syndromes, Conditions Not Attributable to a Mental Disorder That Are a Focus of Attention or Treatment, and Additional Codes

Axis II Personality Disorders and Specific Developmental Disorders

Axis III Physical Disorders and Conditions

Axes IV and V are available for use in special clinical and research settings and provide information supplementing the official DSM-III diagnoses (Axes I, II, and III) that may be useful for planning treatment and predicting outcome:

Axis IV Severity of Psychosocial Stressors

Axis V Highest Level of Adaptive Functioning Past Year

Use of the DSM-III multiaxial classification ensures that attention is given to certain types of disorders, aspects of the environment, and areas of functioning that might be overlooked if the focus were on assessing a single presenting problem.

Axes I and II

Axes I and II comprise the entire classification of mental disorders plus Conditions Not Attributable to a Mental Disorder That Are a Focus of Attention or Treatment. The disorders listed on Axis II are the Personality Disorders (for adults and, in some cases, for children and adolescents) and the Specific Developmental Disorders (for children and adolescents and, in some cases, for adults). The remaining disorders and conditions are included in Axis I. This separation ensures that consideration is given to the possible presence of disorders that are frequently overlooked when attention is directed to the usually more florid Axis I disorder.

In some instances an individual may have a disorder on both axes. For example, an adult may have Major Depression noted on Axis I and Compulsive Personality Disorder on Axis II, or a child may have Conduct Disorder noted on Axis I and Developmental Language Disorder on Axis II. In other instances there may be no disorder on Axis I, the reason for seeking treatment being limited to a condition noted on Axis II. In this latter case, the clinician should write: *Axis I:* V71.09 No diagnosis or condition on Axis I. On the other hand, if a disorder is noted on Axis I but there is no evidence of an Axis II disorder, the clinician should write: *Axis II:* V71.09 No diagnosis on Axis II, or one of the Conditions Not Attributable to a Mental Disorder That Are a Focus of Attention or Treatment should be recorded.

Multiple diagnoses within Axes I and II

On both Axes I and II, multiple diagnoses should be made when necessary to describe the current condition. This applies particularly to Axis I, in which, for example, an individual may have both a Substance Use Disorder and an Affective Disorder. It is possible to have multiple diagnoses within the same class. For example, it is possible to have several Substance Use Disorders or, in the class of Affective Disorders, it is possible to have Major Depression superimposed on Dysthymic Disorder or Bipolar Disorder superimposed on Cyclothymic Disorder. In other classes, such as Schizophrenic Disorders, however, each of the subtypes is mutually exclusive.

Within Axis II, diagnosis of multiple Specific Developmental Disorders is common. For some adults the persistence of a Specific Developmental Disorder and the presence of a Personality Disorder may require that both be noted on Axis II. Usually, a single Personality Disorder will be noted; but when the individual meets the criteria for more than one, all should be recorded.

Axis II and description of personality features

Axis II can be used to indicate specific personality traits when no Personality Disorder exists. For example, compulsive traits can be recorded on Axis

II for an individual for whom Major Depression is noted on Axis I. Even when a Personality Disorder is noted on Axis II, the clinician may wish to indicate other personality characteristics—e.g., paranoid traits can be noted on Axis II for an individual who is also described as having Compulsive Personality Disorder on this same axis. (Code numbers should not be used when personality *traits* are noted, since a code number indicates a Personality *Disorder*.)

Principal diagnosis

When an individual receives more than one diagnosis, the *principal* diagnosis is the condition that was chiefly responsible for occasioning the evaluation or admission to clinical care. In most cases this condition will be the main focus of attention or treatment. The principal diagnosis may be an Axis I or an Axis II diagnosis; but when an Axis II diagnosis is the principal diagnosis, the notation should be followed by the phrase "(Principal diagnosis)". Example:

Axis I:	303.93	Alcohol Dependence, In Remission
Axis II:	301.70	Antisocial Personality Disorder (Principal diagnosis)

When an individual has both an Axis I and an Axis II diagnosis, the principal diagnosis will be assumed to be on Axis I unless the Axis II diagnosis is followed by the qualifying phrase "(Principal diagnosis)".

When multiple diagnoses are made on either Axis I or Axis II, they should be listed within each axis in the order of focus of attention or treatment. For example, if an individual with Schizophrenia, Paranoid Type, Chronic, comes to an emergency room for treatment of Alcohol Intoxication, the diagnosis should be listed:

Axis I:	303.00	Alcohol Intoxication
	295.32	Schizophrenia, Paranoid Type, Chronic

Provisional diagnosis

In some instances not enough information will be available to make a firm diagnosis. The clinician may wish to indicate a significant degree of diagnostic uncertainty by writing "(Provisional)" following the diagnosis—e.g., Schizophreniform Disorder (Provisional, R/O Organic Delusional Syndrome).

Levels of diagnostic certainty

Frequently a diagnostic evaluation yields insufficient information to make a specific diagnosis. The following table indicates the various ways in which a clinician may indicate diagnostic uncertainty:

Term	Examples of clinical situations
V Codes (for Conditions Not Attributable to a Mental Disorder That Are a Focus of Attention or Treatment)	Insufficient information to know whether or not a presenting problem is attributable to a mental disorder, e.g., Academic Problem; Adult Antisocial Behavior.
799.90 Axis I Diagnosis or Condition Deferred	Information inadequate to make any diagnostic judgment about an Axis I diagnosis or condition.
799.90 Axis II Diagnosis Deferred	Same for an Axis II diagnosis.
300.90 Unspecified mental disorder (nonpsychotic)	Enough information available to rule out a psychotic disorder, but further specification is not possible.
298.90 Atypical Psychosis	Enough information available to determine the presence of a psychotic disorder, but further specification is not possible.
Atypical (class of disorder)	Enough information available to indicate the class of disorder that is present, but further specification is not possible, because either there is not sufficient information to make a more specific diagnosis, or the clinical features of the disorder do not meet the criteria for any of the

	other categories, e.g., Atypical Affective Disorder.
Specific diagnosis (Provisional)	Enough information available to make a "working" diagnosis, but the clinician wishes to indicate a significant degree of diagnostic uncertainty, e.g., Schizophreniform Disorder (Provisional).

Axis III. Physical Disorders or Conditions

Axis III permits the clinician to indicate any current physical disorder or condition that is potentially relevant to the understanding or management of the individual. These are the conditions outside of the mental disorders section of ICD-9-CM. In some instances the condition may be etiologically significant (e.g., a neurologic disorder associated with Dementia); in other instances the physical disorder may not be etiologic, but important in the overall management of the individual (e.g., diabetes in a child with Conduct Disorder). In yet other instances, the clinician may wish to note significant associated physical findings, such as "soft neurological signs." Multiple diagnoses are permitted.

Axis IV. Severity of Psychosocial Stressors

Axis IV provides a coding of the overall severity of a stressor judged to have been a significant contributor to the development or exacerbation of the current disorder. An individual's prognosis may be better when a disorder develops as a consequence of a severe stressor than when it develops after no stressor or a minimal stressor.

Rating the severity of the stressor

This should be based on the clinician's assessment of the stress an "average" person in similar circumstances and with similar sociocultural values would experience from the particular psychosocial stressor(s). This judgment involves consideration of the following: the amount of change in the individual's life caused by the stressor, the degree to which the event is desired and under the individual's control, and the number of stressors. Even though a specific stressor may have greater impact on an individual who is especially vulnerable or has certain internal conflicts, the rating should be based on the severity of the stressor itself, not on the individual's vulnerability to the particular stressor. If a vulnerability to stress exists, it will frequently be due to a mental disorder that is coded on Axis I or II.

In most instances the psychosocial stressor will have occurred within a year prior to the current disorder (Post-traumatic Stress Disorder is a notable exception). In some instances the stressor is the anticipation of a future event: for example, the knowledge that one will soon retire. Although a stressor frequently plays a precipitating role in a disorder, it may also be a consequence of the individual's psychopathology—e.g., Alcohol Dependence may lead to marital problems and divorce, which can then become stressors contributing to the development of Major Depression. The current disorder that is related to the psychosocial stressor may be either a clinical syndrome, coded on Axis I, or an exacerbation of a Personality or Specific Developmental Disorder, coded on Axis II.

In addition to the severity rating, in certain settings it may be useful to note the specific psychosocial stressor (e.g., chronic marital discord about sharing household duties). This information may be important in formulating a treatment plan that includes attempts to remove the psychosocial stressor or to help the individual cope with it. More than one psychosocial stressor may be judged etiologically significant by the clinician, but rarely will more than four be recorded. The stressors should be noted as specifically as possible and listed in order of their importance.

The severity rating should reflect the summed effect of all of the psychosocial stressors that are listed. The following codes and terms may be used as guides in making the rating:

Code	Term	Adult examples	Child or adolescent examples
1	None	No apparent psychosocial stressor	No apparent psychosocial stressor
2	Minimal	Minor violation of the law; small bank loan	Vacation with family
3	Mild	Argument with neighbor; change in work hours	Change in school teacher; new school year
4	Moderate	New career; death of close friend; pregnancy	Chronic parental fighting; change to new school; illness of close relative; birth of sibling
5	Severe	Serious illness in self or family; major financial loss; marital separation; birth of child	Death of peer; divorce of parents; arrest; hospitalization; persistent and harsh parental discipline
6	Extreme	Death of close relative; divorce	Death of parent or sibling; repeated physical or sexual abuse

7	Catastrophic	Concentration camp experience; devastating natural disaster	Multiple family deaths
0	Unspecified	No information, or not applicable	No information, or not applicable

Axis V. Highest Level of Adaptive Functioning Past Year

Axis V permits the clinician to indicate his or her judgment of an individual's highest level of adaptive functioning (for at least a few months) during the past year. This information frequently has prognostic significance, because usually an individual returns to his or her previous level of adaptive functioning after an episode of illness.

As conceptualized here, adaptive functioning is a composite of three major areas: social relations, occupational functioning, and use of leisure time. These three areas are to be considered together, although there is evidence that social relations should be given greater weight because of its particularly great prognostic significance. An assessment of the use of leisure time will affect the overall judgment only when there is no significant impairment in social relations and occupational functioning or when occupational opportunities are limited or absent (e.g., the individual is retired or handicapped).

Social relations includes all relations with people, with particular emphasis on family and friends. The breadth and quality of interpersonal relationships should be considered.

Occupational functioning refers to functioning as a worker, student, or homemaker. The amount, complexity, and quality of the work accomplished should be considered. The highest levels of adaptive functioning should be used only when high occupational productivity is not associated with a high level of subjective discomfort.

Use of leisure time includes recreational activities or hobbies. The range and depth of involvement and the pleasure derived should be considered.

The level noted should be descriptive of the individual's functioning regardless of whether or not special circumstances, such as concurrent treatment, may have been necessary to sustain that level.

Examples of How To Record the Results of a DSM-III Multiaxial Evaluation

Example 1:

Axis I:	296.23	Major Depression, Single Episode, With Melancholia
	303.93	Alcohol Dependence, In Remission
Axis II:	301.60	Dependent Personality Disorder (Provisional, R/O Borderline Personality Disorder)
Axis III:	Alcoholic cirrhosis of the liver	
Axis IV:	Psychosocial stressors: anticipated retirement and change in residence with loss of contact with friends Severity: 4—Moderate	
Axis V:	Highest level of adaptive functioning past year: 3—Good	

Example 2:

Axis I:	304.03	Heroin Dependence, In Remission
Axis II:	301.70	Antisocial Personality Disorder (Principal diagnosis); prominent paranoid traits
Axis III:	None	
Axis IV:	Psychosocial stressors: No information Severity: 0—Unspecified	
Axis V:	Highest level of adaptive functioning past year: 5—Poor	

Example 3:

Axis I:	295.92	Schizophrenia, Undifferentiated Type, Chronic
	V62.89	Borderline Intellectual Functioning (Provisional)
Axis II:	V71.09	No diagnosis of Axis II

Levels	Adult examples	Child or adolescent examples
1 **SUPERIOR**—Unusually effective functioning in social relations, occupational functioning, and use of leisure time.	Single parent living in deteriorating neighborhood takes excellent care of children and home, has warm relations with friends, and finds time for pursuit of hobby.	12-year-old girl gets superior grades in school, is extremely popular among her peers, and excels in many sports. She does all of this with apparent ease and comfort.
2 **VERY GOOD**—Better than average functioning in social relations, occupational functioning, and use of leisure time.	A 65-year-old retired widower does some volunteer work, often sees old friends, and pursues hobbies.	An adolescent boy gets excellent grades, works part time, has several close friends, and plays banjo in the jazz band. He admits to some distress in "keeping up with everything."
3 **GOOD**—No more than slight impairment in either social or occupational functioning.	A woman with many friends functions extremely well at a difficult job, but says "the strain is too much."	An 8-year-old boy does well in school, has several friends, but bullies younger children.

4 **FAIR**—Moderate impairment in either social relations or occupational functioning, or some impairment in both.	A lawyer has trouble carrying through assignments, has several acquaintances, but hardly any close friends.	A 10-year-old girl does poorly in school, but has adequate peer and family relations.
5 **POOR**—Marked impairment in either social relations or occupational functioning, or moderate impairment in both.	A man with one or two friends has trouble keeping a job for more than a few weeks.	A 14-year-old boy almost fails in school and has trouble getting along with his peers.
6 **VERY POOR**—Marked impairment in both social relations and occupational functioning.	A woman is unable to do any of her housework and has violent outbursts toward family and neighbors.	A 6-year-old girl needs special help in all subjects and has virtually no peer relationships.
7 **GROSSLY IMPAIRED**—Gross impairment in virtually all areas of functioning.	An elderly man needs supervision to maintain minimal personal hygiene and is usually incoherent.	A 4-year-old boy needs constant restraint to avoid hurting himself and is almost totally lacking in language skills.
0 **UNSPECIFIED**	No information.	No information.

Axis III: Late effects of viral encephalitis

Axis IV: Psychosocial stressors: death of mother
Severity: 6—Extreme

Axis V: Highest level of adaptive functioning past year: 6—Very poor

DIAGNOSTIC CRITERIA

Diagnostic criteria appear at the end of the text describing each specific diagnosis.

These criteria are offered as useful guides for making the diagnosis, since it has been demonstrated that the use of such criteria enhances diagnostic agreement among clinicians. It should, however, be understood that for most of the categories the criteria are based on clinical judgment, and have not yet been fully validated; with further experience and study, the criteria will, in many cases, undoubtedly be revised.

Designation by capital letters indicates multiple criteria, the presence of *all* of which constitutes the guide to making the diagnosis.

EXPLANATION OF TERMS AND CONVENTIONS

Atypical. This term is used to indicate a category within a class of disorders that is residual to the specific categories in that class, although it is recognized that in some settings what is regarded as an atypical disorder may actually be more common than any of the specific disorders in that particular class. (In the literature the term "atypical" has sometimes been used in a different sense—to describe a specific diagnostic category that has unusual features.)

Physical disorders. The term "physical disorders" is used to refer to any disorder listed in ICD-9-CM outside the chapter on mental disorders.

Terms in parentheses. In order to facilitate the identification of the categories that in DSM-II were grouped together in the class of Neuroses, the DSM-

II terms are included separately in parentheses after the corresponding categories. These DSM-II terms are included in ICD-9-CM and therefore are acceptable as alternatives to the recommended DSM-III terms that precede them.

Not due to another disorder. This phrase is used to indicate that the disorder being described is not diagnosed if the disturbance is apparently symptomatic of another disorder. For example, in the diagnostic criteria for Schizophrenia, there is the phrase, "Not due to any Organic Mental Disorder." This means that the diagnosis of Schizophrenia is not given if the characteristic symptoms, such as delusions or hallucinations, are caused by an Organic Mental Disorder.

The Diagnostic Categories

Disorders Usually First Evident in Infancy, Childhood, or Adolescence

This section lists conditions that are usually first evident in infancy, childhood, or adolescence. However, any appropriate adult diagnosis can be used for diagnosing a child.

MENTAL RETARDATION

Differential diagnosis. Specific Developmental Disorders, Pervasive Developmental Disorders, Borderline Intellectual Functioning (V code).

Diagnostic criteria.

A. Significantly subaverage general intellectual functioning: an IQ of 70 or below on an individually administered IQ test (for infants, since available intelligence tests do not yield numerical values, a clinical judgment of significant subaverage intellectual functioning).

B. Concurrent deficits or impairments in adaptive behavior, the person's age being taken into consideration.

C. Onset before the age of 18.

Subtypes. There are four subtypes, reflecting the degree of intellectual impairment and designated as Mild, Moderate, Severe, and Profound. IQ levels to be used as guides for distinguishing the four subtypes are given below:

Subtypes of Mental Retardation		IQ Levels
317.0	Mild Mental Retardation	50-70
318.0	Moderate Mental Retardation	35-49
318.1	Severe Mental Retardation	20-34
318.2	Profound Mental Retardation	Below 20

319.0 Unspecified Mental Retardation

This category should be used when there is a strong presumption of Mental Retardation but the individual is untestable by standard intelligence tests. This may be the case when children, adolescents or adults are too impaired or uncooperative to be tested. In the case of infants, since the available tests, such as the Bayley, Cattel, and others, do not yield numerical IQ values, this may be the case when there is a clinical judgment of significant subaverage intellectual functioning. In general, the younger the age, the more difficult it is to make a diagnosis of Mental Retardation, except for those with profound impairment.

This category should not be used when the intellectual level is presumed to be above 70 (see V code, for Borderline Intellectual Functioning, p. 156).

ATTENTION DEFICIT DISORDER

314.01 Attention Deficit Disorder with Hyperactivity

Differential diagnosis. Age-appropriate overactivity; inadequate, disorganized, or chaotic environments; Severe or Profound Mental Retardation; Conduct Disorder; Schizophrenia; Affective Disorders with manic features.

Diagnostic criteria.

The child displays, for his or her mental and chronological age, signs of developmentally inappropriate inattention, impulsivity, and hyperactivity. The signs must be reported by adults in the child's environment, such as parents and teachers. Because the symptoms are typically variable, they may not be observed directly by the clinician. When the reports of teachers and parents conflict, primary consideration should be given to the teacher reports because of greater familiarity with age-appropriate norms. Symptoms typically worsen in situations that require self-application, as in the classroom. Signs of the disorder may be absent when the child is in a new or a one-to-one situation.

The number of symptoms specified is for children between the ages of eight and ten, the peak age range for referral. In younger children, more severe forms of the symptoms and a greater number of symptoms are usually present. The opposite is true of older children.

A. **Inattention.** At least three of the following:

(1) often fails to finish things he or she starts
(2) often doesn't seem to listen
(3) easily distracted
(4) has difficulty concentrating on schoolwork or other tasks requiring sustained attention
(5) has difficulty sticking to a play activity

B. **Impulsivity.** At least three of the following:

(1) often acts before thinking
(2) shifts excessively from one activity to another
(3) has difficulty organizing work (this not being due to cognitive impairment)
(4) needs a lot of supervision
(5) frequently calls out in class
(6) has difficulty awaiting turn in games or group situations

C. **Hyperactivity.** At least two of the following:

(1) excessively runs about or climbs on things
(2) has difficulty sitting still or fidgets excessively
(3) has difficulty staying seated
(4) moves about excessively during sleep
(5) is always "on the go" or acts as if "driven by a motor"

D. Onset before the age of seven.

E. Duration of at least six months.

F. Not due to Schizophrenia, Affective Disorder, or Severe or Profound Mental Retardation.

314.00 Attention Deficit Disorder without Hyperactivity

Diagnostic criteria.

The criteria for this disorder are the same as those for Attention Deficit Disorder with Hyperactivity except that the individual never had signs of hyperactivity (criterion C).

314.80 Attention Deficit Disorder, Residual Type

Diagnostic criteria.

A. The individual once met the criteria for Attention Deficit Disorder with Hyperactivity. This information may come from the individual or from others, such as family members.

B. Signs of hyperactivity are no longer present, but other signs of the illness have persisted to the present without periods of remission, as evidenced by signs of both attentional deficits and impulsivity (e.g., difficulty organizing work and completing tasks, difficulty concentrating, being easily distracted, making sudden decisions without thought of the consequences).

C. The symptoms of inattention and impulsivity result in some impairment in social or occupational functioning.

D. Not due to Schizophrenia, Affective Disorder, or Severe or Profound Mental Retardation.

CONDUCT DISORDER

Differential diagnosis. Isolated acts of antisocial behavior (Childhood or Adolescent Antisocial Behavior —V codes), Oppositional Disorder.

312.00 Conduct Disorder, Undersocialized, Aggressive

A. A repetitive and persistent pattern of aggressive conduct in which the basic rights of others are violated, as manifested by either of the following:

(1) physical violence against persons or property (not to defend someone else or oneself), e.g., vandalism, rape, breaking and entering, fire-setting, mugging, assault
(2) thefts outside the home involving confrontation with the victim (e.g., extortion, purse-snatching, gas station robbery)

B. Failure to establish a normal degree of affection, empathy, or bond with others as evidenced by *no more than one* of the following indications of social attachment:

(1) has one or more peer-group friendships that have lasted over six months
(2) extends himself or herself for others even when no immediate advantage is likely
(3) apparently feels guilt or remorse when such a reaction is appropriate (not just when caught or in difficulty)
(4) avoids blaming or informing on companions
(5) shares concern for the welfare of friends or companions

C. Duration of pattern of aggressive conduct of at least six months.

D. If 18 or older, does not meet the criteria for Antisocial Personality Disorder.

312.10 Conduct Disorder, Undersocialized, Nonaggressive

Diagnostic criteria.

A. A repetitive and persistent pattern of nonaggressive conduct in which either the basic rights of others or major age-appropriate societal norms or rules are violated, as manifested by any of the following:

(1) chronic violations of a variety of important rules (that are reasonable and age-appropriate for the child) at home or at school (e.g., persistent truancy, substance abuse)
(2) repeated running away from home overnight
(3) persistent serious lying in and out of the home
(4) stealing not involving confrontation with a victim

B. Failure to establish a normal degree of affection, empathy, or bond with others as evidenced by *no more than one* of the following indications of social attachment:

(1) has one or more peer-group friendships that have lasted over six months
(2) extends himself or herself for others even

when no immediate advantage is likely
(3) apparently feels guilt or remorse when such a reaction is appropriate (not just when caught or in difficulty)
(4) avoids blaming or informing on companions
(5) shows concern for the welfare of friends or companions

C. Duration of pattern of nonaggressive conduct of at least six months.

D. If 18 or older, does not meet the criteria for Antisocial Personality Disorder.

312.23 Conduct Disorder, Socialized, Aggressive

Diagnostic criteria.

A. A repetitive and persistent pattern of aggressive conduct in which the basic rights of others are violated, as manifested by either of the following:

(1) physical violence against persons or property (not to defend someone else or oneself), e.g., vandalism, rape, breaking and entering, fire-setting, mugging, assault
(2) thefts outside the home involving confrontation with a victim (e.g., extortion, purse-snatching, gas station robbery)

B. Evidence of social attachment to others as indicated by at least two of the following behavior patterns:

(1) has one or more peer-group friendships that have lasted over six months
(2) extends himself or herself for others even when no immediate advantage is likely
(3) apparently feels guilt or remorse when such a reaction is appropriate (not just when caught or in difficulty)
(4) avoids blaming or informing on companions
(5) shows concern for the welfare of friends or companions

C. Duration of pattern of aggressive conduct of at least six months.

D. If 18 or older, does not meet the criteria for Antisocial Personality Disorder.

312.21 Conduct Disorder, Socialized, Nonaggressive

Diagnostic criteria.

A. A repetitive and persistent pattern of nonaggressive conduct in which either the basic rights of others or major age-appropriate societal norms or rules are violated, as manifested by any of the following:

(1) chronic violations of a variety of important rules (that are reasonable and age-appropriate for the child) at home or at school (e.g., persistent truancy, substance abuse)
(2) repeated running away from home overnight
(3) persistent serious lying in and out of the home
(4) stealing not involving confrontation with a victim

B. Evidence of social attachment to others as indicated by at least two of the following behavior patterns:

(1) has one or more peer-group friendships that have lasted over six months
(2) extends himself or herself for others even when no immediate advantage is likely
(3) apparently feels guilt or remorse when such a reaction is appropriate (not just when caught or in difficulty)
(4) avoids blaming or informing on companions
(5) shows concern for the welfare of friends or companions

C. Duration of pattern of nonaggressive conduct of at least six months.

D. If 18 or older, does not meet the criteria for Antisocial Personality Disorder.

312.90 Atypical Conduct Disorder

This is a residual category for illnesses in which the predominant disturbance involves a pattern of conduct in which there is violation of either the basic rights of others or major age-appropriate societal norms or rules but which cannot be classified as one of the specified Conduct Disorder subtypes.

ANXIETY DISORDERS OF CHILDHOOD OR ADOLESCENCE

309.21 Separation Anxiety Disorder

Differential diagnosis. Overanxious Disorder, Avoidant Disorder of Childhood or Adolescence, Pervasive Developmental Disorders, Schizophrenia, Major Depression, Conduct Disorder with truancy, Phobic Disorder.

Diagnostic criteria.

A. Excessive anxiety concerning separation from those to whom the child is attached, as manifested by at least three of the following:

(1) unrealistic worry about possible harm befalling major attachment figures or fear that they will leave and will not return

(2) unrealistic worry that an untoward calamitous event will separate the child from a major attachment figure, e.g., the child will be lost, kidnapped, killed, or be the victim of an accident

(3) persistent reluctance or refusal to go to school in order to stay with major attachment figures or at home

(4) persistent reluctance or refusal to go to sleep without being next to a major attachment figure or to go to sleep away from home

(5) persistent avoidance of being alone in the home and emotional upset if unable to follow the major attachment figure around the home

(6) repeated nightmares involving theme of separation

(7) complaints of physical symptoms on school days, e.g., stomachaches, headaches, nausea, vomiting

(8) signs of excessive distress upon separation, or when anticipating separation, from major attachment figures, e.g., temper tantrums or crying, pleading with parents not to leave (for children below the age of six, the distress must be of panic proportions)

(9) social withdrawal, apathy, sadness or difficulty concentrating on work or play when not with a major attachment figure

B. Duration of disturbance of at least two weeks.

C. Not due to a Pervasive Developmental Disorder, Schizophrenia, or any other psychotic disorder.

D. If 18 or older, does not meet the criteria for Agoraphobia.

313.21 Avoidant Disorder of Childhood or Adolescence

Differential diagnosis. Age-appropriate social reticence in young children, Separation Anxiety Disorder, Overanxious Disorder, Schizoid Disorder of Childhood or Adolescence, Avoidant Personality Disorder, Adjustment Disorder with Withdrawal.

Diagnostic criteria.

A. Persistent and excessive shrinking from contact with strangers.

B. Desire for affection and acceptance, and generally warm and satisfying relations with family members and other familiar figures.

C. Avoidant behavior sufficiently severe to interfere with social functioning in peer relationships.

D. Age at least 2½. If 18 or older, does not meet the criteria for Avoidant Personality Disorder.

E. Duration of the disturbance of at least six months.

313.00 Overanxious Disorder

Differential diagnosis. Separation Anxiety Disorder, Avoidant Disorder of Childhood or Adolescence, Attention Deficit Disorder, Adjustment Disorder with Anxious Mood, Obsessive Compulsive Disorder,

Major Depression, Schizophrenia, Pervasive Developmental Disorders.

Diagnostic criteria.

A. The predominant disturbance is generalized and persistent anxiety or worry (not related to concerns about separation), as manifested by at least four of the following:

(1) unrealistic worry about future events
(2) preoccupation with the appropriateness of the individual's behavior in the past
(3) overconcern about competence in a variety of areas, e.g., academic, athletic, social
(4) excessive need for reassurance about a variety of worries
(5) somatic complaints, such as headaches or stomachaches, for which no physical basis can be established
(6) marked self-consciousness or susceptibility to embarrassment or humiliation
(7) marked feeling of tension or inability to relax

B. The symptoms in A have persisted for at least six months.

C. If 18 or older, does not meet the criteria for Generalized Anxiety Disorder.

D. The disturbance is not due to another mental disorder, such as Separation Anxiety Disorder, Avoidant Disorder of Childhood or Adolescence, Phobic Disorder, Obsessive Compulsive Disorder, Depressive Disorder, Schizophrenia, or a Pervasive Developmental Disorder.

OTHER DISORDERS OF INFANCY, CHILDHOOD OR ADOLESCENCE

313.89 Reactive Attachment Disorder of Infancy

Differential diagnosis. Severe neurological abnormalities, such as deafness, blindness, profound multisensory defects; severe chronic physical illness; psychosocial dwarfism; Mental Retardation; Infantile Autism; Major Depression.

Diagnostic criteria.

A. Age at onset before eight months.

B. Lack of the type of care that ordinarily leads to the development of affectional bonds to others, e.g., gross emotional neglect, imposed social isolation in an institution.

C. Lack of developmentally appropriate signs of social responsivity, as indicated by at least several of the following (the total number of behaviors looked for will depend on the chronological age of the child, corrected for prematurity):

(1) lack of visual tracking of eyes and faces by an infant more than two months of age
(2) lack of smiling in response to faces by an infant more than two months of age
(3) lack of visual reciprocity in an infant of more than two months; lack of vocal reciprocity with caretaker in an infant of more than five months
(4) lack of alerting and turning toward caretaker's voice by an infant of more than four months
(5) lack of spontaneous reaching for the mother by an infant of more than four months
(6) lack of anticipatory reaching when approached to be picked up by an infant more than five months of age
(7) lack of participation in playful games with caretaker by an infant of more than five months

D. At least three of the following:

(1) weak cry
(2) excessive sleep
(3) lack of interest in the environment
(4) hypomotility
(5) poor muscle tone
(6) weak rooting and grasping in response to feeding attempts

E. Weight loss or failure to gain appropriate amount of weight for age unexplainable by any physical disorder. In these cases usually the failure to gain weight (falling weight percentile) is disproportionately greater than failure to gain length; head circumference is normal.

F. Not due to a physical disorder, Mental Retardation, or Infantile Autism.

G. The diagnosis is confirmed if the clinical picture is reversed shortly after institution of adequate caretaking, which frequently includes short-term hospitalization.

313.22 Schizoid Disorder of Childhood or Adolescence

Differential diagnosis. Avoidant Disorder of Childhood or Adolescence; Schizophrenia; Pervasive Developmental Disorders; Conduct Disorder, Undersocialized, Nonaggressive.

Diagnostic criteria.

A. No close friend of similar age other than a relative or a similarly socially isolated child.

B. No apparent interest in making friends.

C. No pleasure from usual peer interactions.

D. General avoidance of nonfamilial social contacts, especially with peers.

E. No interest in activities that involve other children (such as team sports, clubs).

F. Duration of the disturbance of at least three months.

G. Not due to Pervasive Developmental Disorder; Conduct Disorder, Undersocialized, Nonaggressive, or any psychotic disorder, such as Schizophrenia.

H. If 18 or older, does not meet the criteria for Schizoid Personality Disorder.

313.23 Elective Mutism

Differential diagnosis. Refusal to speak in children in families who have immigrated to a country of a different language, Severe or Profound Mental Retardation, Pervasive Developmental Disorders, Developmental Language Disorder, Major Depression,

Avoidant Disorder of Childhood or Adolescence, Overanxious Disorder, Oppositional Disorder, Social Phobia.

Diagnostic criteria.

A. Continuous refusal to talk in almost all social situations, including at school.

B. Ability to comprehend spoken language and to speak.

C. Not due to another mental or physical disorder.

313.81 Oppositional Disorder

Differential diagnosis. Normal oppositional behavior in 18-to-36-month-old children, Conduct Disorder, Schizophrenia, Pervasive Developmental Disorders, Attention Deficit Disorder, Mental Retardation, chronic Organic Mental Disorders.

Diagnostic criteria.

A. Onset after 3 years of age and before age 18.

B. A pattern, for at least six months, of disobedient, negativistic, and provocative opposition to authority figures, as manifested by at least two of the following symptoms:

(1) violations of minor rules
(2) temper tantrums
(3) argumentativeness
(4) provocative behavior
(5) stubbornness

C. No violation of the basic rights of others or of major age-appropriate societal norms or rules (as in Conduct Disorder), and the disturbance is not due to another mental disorder, such as Schizophrenia or a Pervasive Developmental Disorder.

D. If 18 or older, does not meet the criteria for Passive-Aggressive Personality Disorder.

313.82 Identity Disorder

Differential diagnosis. Normal conflicts associated with maturing, Schizophrenia, Schizophreniform Disorder, Affective Disorder, Borderline Personality Disorder.

Diagnostic criteria.

A. Severe subjective distress regarding uncertainty about a variety of issues relating to identity, including three or more of the following:

(1) long-term goals
(2) career choice
(3) friendship patterns
(4) sexual orientation and behavior
(5) religious identification
(6) moral value systems
(7) group loyalties

B. Impairment in social or occupational (including academic) functioning as a result of the symptoms in A.

C. Duration of the disturbance of at least three months.

D. Not due to another mental disorder, such as Affective Disorder, Schizophrenia, or Schizophreniform Disorder.

E. If 18 or older, does not meet the criteria for Borderline Personality Disorder.

EATING DISORDERS

307.10 Anorexia Nervosa

Differential diagnosis. Physical disorders with weight loss, Bulimia, Depressive Disorders, Schizophrenia with bizarre eating patterns.

Diagnostic criteria.

A. Intense fear of becoming obese, which does not diminish as weight loss progresses.

B. Disturbance of body image, e.g., claiming to "feel fat" even when emaciated.

C. Weight loss of at least 25% of original body weight or, if under 18 years of age, weight loss from original body weight plus projected weight gain expected from growth charts may be combined to make the 25%.

D. Refusal to maintain body weight over a minimal normal weight for age and height.

E. No known physical illness that would account for the weight loss.

307.51 Bulimia

Differential diagnosis. Certain neurological diseases, such as epileptic equivalent seizures, CNS tumors, Klüver-Bucy-like syndromes, or Klein-Levin syndrome; Anorexia Nervosa; Schizophrenia with unusual eating behavior.

Diagnostic criteria.

A. Recurrent episodes of binge eating (rapid consumption of a large amount of food in a discrete period of time, usually less than two hours).

B. At least three of the following:

(1) consumption of high-caloric, easily ingested food during a binge

(2) unconspicuous eating during a binge

(3) termination of such eating episodes by abdominal pain, sleep, social interruption, or self-induced vomiting

(4) repeated attempts to lose weight by severely restrictive diets, self-induced vomiting, or use of cathartics and/or diuretics

(5) frequent weight fluctuations greater than ten pounds due to alternating binges and fasts

C. Awareness that the eating pattern is abnormal and fear of not being able to stop eating voluntarily.

D. Depressed mood and self-deprecating thoughts following eating binges.

E. The bulimic episodes are not due to Anorexia Nervosa or any known physical disorder.

307.52 Pica

Differential diagnosis. Certain physical disorders, such as Klein-Levin syndrome; Infantile Autism; Schizophrenia with bizarre eating behavior.

Diagnostic criteria.

A. Repeated eating of a nonnutritive substance for at least one month.

B. Not due to another mental disorder, such as Infantile Autism or Schizophrenia, or a physical disorder, such as Klein-Levin syndrome.

307.53 Rumination Disorder of Infancy

Differential diagnosis. Congenital anomalies, such as pyloric stenosis; infections of the gastrointestinal system.

Diagnostic criteria.

A. Repeated regurgitation without nausea or associated gastrointestinal illness for at least one month following a period of normal functioning.

B. Weight loss or failure to make expected weight gain.

307.50 Atypical Eating Disorder

This category is a residual category for eating disorders that cannot be adequately classified in any of the previous categories.

STEREOTYPED MOVEMENT DISORDERS

Differential diagnosis of tics. Choreiform, dystonic, athetoid, myoclonic and hemiballismic movements;

spasms such as hemifacial spasm; synkinesis; dyskinesias.

307.21 Transient Tic Disorder

Differential diagnosis. Tourette's Disorder, Chronic Motor Tic Disorder.

Diagnostic criteria.

A. Onset during childhood.

B. Presence of recurrent, involuntary, repetitive, rapid, purposeless motor movements (tics).

C. Ability to suppress the movements voluntarily for minutes to hours.

D. Variation in the intensity of the symptoms over weeks or months.

E. Duration of at least one month but not more than one year.

307.22 Chronic Motor Tic Disorder

Differential diagnosis. Transient Tic Disorder, Tourette's Disorder.

Diagnostic criteria.

A. Presence of recurrent, involuntary, repetitive, rapid, purposeless motor movements (tics) involving no more than three muscle groups at any one time.

B. Unvarying intensity of the tics over weeks or months.

C. Ability to suppress the movements voluntarily for minutes to hours.

D. Duration of at least one year.

307.23 Tourette's Disorder

Differential diagnosis. Abnormal motor movements associated with cerebrovascular accidents, multiple sclerosis, general paresis, Amphetamine Intoxication, Lesch-Nyhan syndrome, Wilson's disease, Sydenham's and Huntington's chorea, Schizophrenia, Organic Mental Disorders.

Diagnostic criteria.

A. Age at onset between 2 and 15 years.

B. Presence of recurrent, involuntary, repetitive, rapid, purposeless motor movements affecting multiple muscle groups.

C. Multiple vocal tics.

D. Ability to suppress movements voluntarily for minutes to hours.

E. Variations in the intensity of the symptoms over weeks or months.

F. Duration of more than one year.

307.20 Atypical Tic Disorder

This category is for the diagnosis of tics that cannot be adequately classified in any of the previous categories.

307.30 Atypical Stereotyped Movement Disorder

This category is for conditions such as head banging, rocking, repetitive hand movements consisting of quick, rhythmic, small hand rotations, or repetitive voluntary movements that typically involve the fingers or arms. These disorders are distinguishable from tics in that they consist of voluntary movements and are not spasmodic.

OTHER DISORDERS WITH PHYSICAL MANIFESTATIONS

307.00 Stuttering

Differential diagnosis. Spastic dysphonia, cluttering.

Diagnostic criteria.

Frequent repetitions or prolongations of sounds, syllables, or words or frequent, unusual hesitations and pauses that disrupt the rhythmic flow of speech.

307.60 Functional Enuresis

Differential diagnosis. Organic causes of enuresis, such as diabetes and seizure disorder.

Diagnostic criteria.

A. Repeated involuntary voiding of urine by day or at night.

B. At least two such events per month for children between the ages of five and six, and at least one event per month for older children.

C. Not due to a physical disorder, such as diabetes or a seizure disorder.

307.70 Functional Encopresis

Differential diagnosis. Organic causes of encopresis such as aganglionic megacolon, anal fissure.

Diagnostic criteria.

A. Repeated, voluntary or involuntary passage of feces of normal or near-normal consistency into places not appropriate for that purpose in the individual's own sociocultural setting.

B. At least one such event a month after the age of four.

C. Not due to a physical disorder, such as aganglionic megacolon.

307.46 Sleepwalking Disorder

Differential diagnosis. Psychomotor epileptic seizures, sleep drunkenness, Psychogenic Fugue.

Diagnostic criteria.

A. There are repeated episodes of arising from bed during sleep and walking about for several minutes to a half hour, usually occurring between 30 and 200 minutes after onset of sleep (the interval of sleep that typically contains EEG delta activity, sleep stages 3 and 4).

B. While sleepwalking, the individual has a blank, staring face; is relatively unresponsive to the efforts of others to influence the sleepwalking or to communicate with him or her; and can be wakened only with great difficulty.

C. Upon awakening (either from the sleepwalking episode or the next morning), the individual has amnesia for the route traversed and for what happened during the episode.

D. Within several minutes of awakening from the sleepwalking episode, there is no impairment of mental activity or behavior (although there may initially be a short period of confusion or disorientation).

E. There is no evidence that the episode occurred during REM sleep or that there is abnormal electrical brain activity during sleep.

307.46 Sleep Terror Disorder

Differential diagnosis. REM sleep nightmares, hypnagogic hallucinations, epileptic seizures.

A. Repeated episodes of abrupt awakening (lasting 1-10 minutes) from sleep, usually occurring between 30 and 200 minutes after onset of sleep (the interval of sleep that typically contains EEG delta activity, sleep stages 3 and 4) and usually beginning with a panicky scream.

B. Intense anxiety during the episode and at least three of the following signs of autonomic arousal:

(1) tachycardia
(2) rapid breathing
(3) dilated pupils
(4) sweating
(5) piloerection

C. Relative unresponsiveness to efforts of others to comfort the individual during the episode and, almost invariably, confusion, disorientation, and perseverative motor movements (e.g., picking at pillow).

D. No evidence that the episode occurred during REM sleep or of abnormal electrical brain activity during sleep.

PERVASIVE DEVELOPMENTAL DISORDERS

299.0x Infantile Autism

Differential diagnosis. Hearing impairment; Mental Retardation; Childhood Onset Pervasive Developmental Disorder; Developmental Language Disorder, Receptive Type; Schizophrenia.

Diagnostic criteria.

A. Onset before 30 months.

B. Pervasive lack of responsiveness to other people (autism).

C. Gross deficits in language development.

D. If speech is present, peculiar speech patterns such as immediate and delayed echolalia, metaphorical language, pronominal reversal.

E. Bizarre responses to various aspects of the environment, e.g., resistance to change, peculiar interest in or attachments to animate or inanimate objects.

F. Absence of delusions, hallucinations, loosening of associations, and incoherence as in Schizophrenia.

299.00 Infantile Autism, Full Syndrome Present

Diagnostic criteria.

Currently meets the criteria for Infantile Autism.

299.01 Infantile Autism, Residual State

Diagnostic criteria.

A. The child once had an illness that met the criteria for Infantile Autism.

B. The current clinical picture no longer meets the full criteria for Infantile Autism, but signs of the illness have persisted to the present, such as oddities of communication and social awkwardness.

299.9x Childhood Onset Pervasive Developmental Disorder

Differential diagnosis. Schizotypal Personality Disorder; See also differential diagnosis of Infantile Autism, p. 43.

Diagnostic criteria.

A. Gross and sustained impairment in social relationships, e.g., lack of appropriate affective responsivity, inappropriate clinging, asociality, lack of empathy.

B. At least three of the following:

(1) sudden excessive anxiety manifested by such symptoms as free-floating anxiety, catastrophic reactions to everyday occurrences, inability to be consoled when upset, unexplained panic attacks
(2) constricted or inappropriate affect, including lack of appropriate fear reactions, unexplained rage reactions, and extreme mood lability
(3) resistance to change in the environment (e.g., upset if dinner time is changed), or insistence on doing things in the same manner every time (e.g., putting on clothes always in the same order)
(4) oddities of motor movement, such as peculiar posturing, peculiar hand or finger movements, or walking on tiptoe
(5) abnormalities of speech, such as questionlike melody, monotonous voice
(6) hyper- or hypo-sensitivity to sensory stimuli, e.g., hyperacusis
(7) self-mutilation, e.g., biting or hitting self, head banging

C. Onset of the full syndrome after 30 months of age and before 12 years of age.

D. Absence of delusions, hallucinations, incoherence, or marked loosening of associations.

299.90 Childhood Onset Pervasive Developmental Disorder, Full Syndrome Present

Diagnostic criteria.

Currently meets the criteria for Childhood Onset Pervasive Developmental Disorder.

299.91 Childhood Onset Pervasive Developmental Disorder, Residual State

Diagnostic criteria.

A. The child once had an illness that met the criteria for Childhood Onset Pervasive Developmental Disorder.

B. The current clinical picture no longer meets the full criteria for the disorder, but signs of the illness have persisted to the present, such as oddities of communication and social awkwardness.

299.8x Atypical Pervasive Developmental Disorder

This category should be used for children with distortions in the development of multiple basic psychological functions that are involved in the development of social skills and language and that cannot be classified as either Infantile Autism or Childhood Onset Pervasive Developmental Disorder.

SPECIFIC DEVELOPMENTAL DISORDERS (Axis II)

315.00 Developmental Reading Disorder

Differential diagnosis. Inadequate schooling, impaired vision or hearing, Mental Retardation.

Diagnostic criterion.

Performance on standardized, individually administered tests of reading skill is significantly below the expected level, given the individual's schooling, chronological age, and mental age (as determined by individually administered IQ test). In addition, in school, the child's performance on tasks requiring reading skills is significantly below his or her intellectual capacity.

315.10 Developmental Arithmetic Disorder

Differential diagnosis. See Developmental Reading Disorder (p. 45).

Diagnostic criteria.

Performance on standardized, individually administered tests of arithmetic achievement is significantly below expected level, given the individual's schooling, chronological age, and mental age (as determined by an individually administered IQ test). In addition, in school, the child's performance on tasks requiring arithmetic skills is significantly below his or her intellectual capacity.

315.31 Developmental Language Disorder
Developmental Language Disorder: Expressive Type

Differential diagnosis. Hearing impairment; Developmental Articulation Disorder; Mental Retardation; acquired aphasia; Infantile Autism; Childhood Onset Pervasive Developmental Disorder.

Diagnostic criteria.

A. Failure to develop vocal expression (encoding) of language despite relatively intact comprehension of language.

B. Presence of inner language (the presence of age-appropriate concepts, such as understanding the purpose and use of a particular household object).

C. Not due to mental Retardation, Childhood Onset Pervasive Developmental Disorder, hearing impairment, or trauma.

Developmental Language Disorder: Receptive Type

Diagnostic criteria.

A. Failure to develop comprehension (decoding) and vocal expression (encoding) of language.

B. Not due to hearing impairment, trauma, Mental Retardation, or Childhood Onset Pervasive Developmental Disorder.

315.39 Developmental Articulation Disorder

Differential diagnosis. Hearing impairment, dysarthria, Developmental Language Disorder, Mental Retardation, Infantile Autism, Childhood Onset Pervasive Developmental Disorder.

Diagnostic criteria.

A. Failure to develop consistent articulations of the later-acquired speech sounds, such as r, sh, th, f, z, l, or ch.

B. Not due to Developmental Language Disorder, Mental Retardation, Childhood Onset Pervasive Developmental Disorder, or physical disorders.

315.50 Mixed Specific Developmental Disorder

The category should be used when there is more than one Specific Developmental Disorder but none is predominant. It is common for a delay in the development of one skill (e.g., reading, arithmetic, or language) to be associated with delays in other skills. The Mixed Specific Developmental Disorder category should be used when the mixture of delayed skills is such that all skills are impaired to relatively the same degree. When the skills are impaired to varying degrees, multiple diagnoses should be recorded, the skill most seriously impaired being recorded first.

315.90 Atypical Specific Developmental Disorder

This is a residual category for use when there is a Specific Developmental Disorder not covered by any of the previous specific categories.

Organic Mental Disorders

ORGANIC BRAIN SYNDROMES

Delirium

Differential diagnosis. Schizophrenia, Schizophreniform Disorder, other psychotic disorders, Dementia, Factitious Disorder with Psychological Symptoms.

Diagnostic criteria.

A. Clouding of consciousness (reduced clarity of awareness of environment), with reduced capacity to shift, focus, and sustain attention to environmental stimuli.

B. At least two of the following:

(1) perceptual disturbance: misinterpretations, illusions, or hallucinations
(2) speech that is at times incoherent
(3) disturbance of sleep-wakefulness cycle with insomnia or daytime drowsiness
(4) increased or decreased psychomotor activity

C. Disorientation and memory impairment (if testable).

D. Clinical features that develop over a short period of time (usually hours to days) and tend to fluctuate over the course of a day.

E. Evidence, from the history, physical examination, or laboratory tests, of a specific organic factor judged to be etiologically related to the disturbance.

Dementia

Differential diagnosis. Normal process of aging, Delirium, Schizophrenia, major depressive episode, Factitious Disorder with Psychological Symptoms.

Diagnostic criteria.

A. A loss of intellectual abilities of sufficient severity to interfere with social or occupational functioning.

B. Memory impairment.

C. At least one of the following:

(1) impairment of abstract thinking, as manifested by concrete interpretation of proverbs, inability to find similarities and differences between related words, difficulty in defining words and concepts, and other similar tasks
(2) impaired judgment
(3) other disturbances of higher cortical function, such as aphasia (disorder of language due to brain dysfunction), apraxia (inability to carry out motor activities despite intact comprehension and motor attention), agnosia (failure to recognize or identify objects despite intact sensory function), "constructional difficulty" (e.g., inability to copy three-dimensional figures, assemble blocks, or arrange sticks in specific designs)
(4) personality change, i.e., alteration or accentuation of premorbid traits

D. State of consciousness not clouded (i.e., does not meet the criteria for Delirium or Intoxication, although these may be superimposed).

E. Either (1) or (2):

(1) there is evidence from either physical examination, medical laboratory tests, or the history of a specific organic factor that is judged to be etiologically related to the disturbance
(2) in the absence of such evidence, an organic factor necessary for the development of the syndrome can be presumed if conditions other than Organic Mental Disorders have been reasonably excluded and if the behavioral change represents cognitive impairment in a variety of areas

Amnestic Syndrome

Differential diagnosis. Delirium, Dementia, Factitious Disorder with Psychological Symptoms.

Diagnostic criteria.

A. Both short-term memory impairment (inability to

learn new information) and long-term memory impairment (inability to remember information that was known in the past) are the predominant clinical features.

B. No clouding of consciousness, as in Delirium and Intoxication, or general loss of major intellectual abilities, as in Dementia.

C. Evidence, from the history, physical examination, or laboratory tests, of a specific organic factor that is judged to be etiologically related to the disturbance.

Organic Delusional Syndrome

Differential diagnosis. Nonorganic psychotic disorders, such as Schizophrenia or Paranoid Disorders; Organic Hallucinosis; Organic Affective Syndrome.

Diagnostic criteria.

A. Delusions are the predominant clinical feature.

B. There is no clouding of consciousness, as in Delirium; there is no significant loss of intellectual abilities, as in Dementia; there are no prominent hallucinations, as in Organic Hallucinosis.

C. There is evidence, from the history, physical examination, or laboratory tests, of a specific organic factor that is judged to be etiologically related to the disturbance.

Organic Hallucinosis

Differential diagnosis. Delirium, Dementia, Organic Delusional Syndrome, Schizophrenia, Affective Disorders, hypnogogic and hypnopompic hallucinations.

Diagnostic criteria.

A. Persistent or recurrent hallucinations are the predominant clinical feature.

B. No clouding of consciousness, as in Delirium; no significant loss of intellectual abilities, as in

Dementia; no predominant disturbance of mood, as in Organic Affective Syndrome; no predominant delusions, as in Organic Delusional Syndrome.

C. Evidence, from the history, physical examination, or laboratory tests, of a specific organic factor that is judged to be etiologically related to the disturbance.

Organic Affective Syndrome

Differential diagnosis. Affective Disorders, Organic Personality Syndrome.

Diagnostic criteria.

A. The predominant disturbance is a disturbance in mood, with at least two of the associated symptoms listed in criterion B for manic or major depressive episode (see p. 95 and p. 98).

B. No clouding of consciousness, as in Delirium; there is no significant loss of intellectual abilities, as in Dementia; there are no predominant delusions or hallucinations, as in Organic Delusional Syndrome or Organic Hallucinosis.

C. Evidence, from the history, physical examination, or laboratory tests, of a specific organic factor that is judged to be etiologically related to the disturbance.

Organic Personality Syndrome

Differential diagnosis. Dementia, Organic Affective Syndrome, Schizophrenia, Paranoid Disorders, Affective Disorders, Disorders of Impulse Control Not Elsewhere Classified.

Diagnostic criteria.

A. A marked change in behavior or personality involving at least one of the following:

(1) emotional lability, e.g., explosive temper

outbursts, sudden crying
(2) impairment in impulse control, e.g., poor social judgment, sexual indiscretions, shoplifting
(3) marked apathy and indifference, e.g., no interest in usual hobbies
(4) suspiciousness or paranoid ideation

B. No clouding of consciousness, as in Delirium; no significant loss of intellectual abilities, as in Dementia; no predominant disturbance of mood, as in Organic Affective Syndrome; no predominant delusions or hallucinations, as in Organic Delusional Syndrome or Organic Hallucinosis.

C. Evidence, from the history, physical examination, or laboratory tests, of a specific organic factor that is judged to be etiologically related to the disturbance.

D. This diagnosis is not given to a child or adolescent if the clinical picture is limited to the features that characterize Attention Deficit Disorder (see p. 24).

Intoxication

Differential diagnosis. Neurological diseases with slurred speech and incoordination, Delirium, Organic Hallucinosis, Organic Delusional Syndrome, Organic Affective Syndrome.

Diagnostic criteria.

A. Development of a substance-specific syndrome that follows the recent ingestion and presence in the body of a substance.

B. Maladaptive behavior during the waking state due to the effect of the substance on the central nervous system, e.g., impaired judgment, belligerence.

C. The clinical picture does not correspond to any of the specific Organic Brain Syndromes, such as Delirium, Organic Delusional Syndrome, Organic Hallucinosis, or Organic Affective Syndrome.

Withdrawal

Differential diagnosis. Physical disorders, such as influenza.

Diagnostic criteria.

A. Development of a substance-specific syndrome that follows the cessation of or reduction in intake of a substance that was previously regularly used by the individual to induce a state of intoxication.

B. The clinical picture does not correspond to any of the specific Organic Brain Syndromes, such as Delirium, Organic Delusional Syndrome, Organic Hallucinosis, or Organic Affective Syndrome.

Atypical or Mixed Organic Brain Syndrome

Diagnostic criteria.

A. The disturbance occurs during the waking state and does not fulfill the criteria for any of the previously described Organic Brain Syndromes.

B. There is evidence, from either physical examination, medical laboratory tests, or history, of a specific organic factor that is judged to be etiologically related to the disturbance.

SECTION 1. Organic Mental Disorders in which the etiology or pathophysiological process is listed below (taken from the mental disorders section of ICD-9-CM).

DEMENTIAS ARISING IN THE SENIUM AND PRESENIUM

290.xx Primary Degenerative Dementia

Differential diagnosis. Normal process of aging, subdural hematoma, normal-pressure hydrocephalus, cerebral neoplasm, Parkinson's disease, vitamin B-12 deficiency, hypothyroidism, substance intoxication, Multi-infarct Dementia, major depressive episode, Dementia, see also Dementia (p. 49).

Diagnostic criteria.

A. Dementia (see p. 49).

B. Insidious onset with uniformly progressive deteriorating course.

C. Exclusion of all other specific causes of Dementia by the history, physical examination, and laboratory tests.

Subtypes

Primary Degenerative Dementia, Senile Onset (after age 65)
290.30 with delirium

290.20 with delusions

290.21 with depression

290.00 uncomplicated

Primary Degenerative Dementia, Presenile Onset (age 65 and below)
290.11 with delirium

290.12 with delusions

290.13 with depression

290.10 uncomplicated

290.4x Multi-infarct Dementia

Differential diagnosis. Single stroke causing aphasia, Primary Degenerative Dementia.

Diagnostic criteria.

A. Dementia (see p. 49).

B. Stepwise deteriorating course (i.e., not uniformly progressive) with "patchy" distribution of deficits (i.e., affecting some functions, but not others) early in the course.

C. Focal neurological signs and symptoms (e.g., exaggeration of deep tendon reflexes, extensor plantar response, pseudobulbar palsy, gait abnormalities, weakness of an extremity, etc.).

D. Evidence, from the history, physical examination, or laboratory tests, of significant cerebrovascular disease that is judged to be etiologically related to the disturbance.

Subtypes

Multi-infarct Dementia

290.41 with delirium

290.42 with delusions

290.43 with depression

290.40 uncomplicated

SUBSTANCE-INDUCED ORGANIC MENTAL DISORDERS

Alcohol Organic Mental Disorders

303.00 Alcohol Intoxication

Differential diagnosis. Social drinking; Intoxication due to barbiturates and similarly acting sedatives and hypnotics; certain neurological diseases, such as cerebellar ataxias or multiple sclerosis; Alcohol Idiosyncratic Intoxication.

Diagnostic criteria.

A. Recent ingestion of alcohol (with no evidence suggesting that the amount was insufficient to cause intoxication in most people).

B. Maladaptive behavioral effects, e.g., fighting, impaired judgment, interference with social or occupational functioning.

C. At least one of the following physiological signs:

(1) slurred speech
(2) incoordination
(3) unsteady gait
(4) nystagmus
(5) flushed face

D. At least one of the following psychological signs:

(1) mood changes
(2) irritability
(3) loquacity
(4) impaired attention

E. Not due to any other physical or mental disorder.

291.40 Alcohol Idiosyncratic Intoxication

Differential diagnosis. Abrupt changes in behavior caused by other exogenous agents, especially barbiturates and similarly acting substances; temporal lobe epilepsy; Malingering.

Diagnostic criteria.

A. Marked behavioral change, e.g., aggressive or assaultive behavior that is due to the recent ingestion of an amount of alcohol insufficient to induce intoxication in most people.

B. The behavior is atypical of the person when not drinking.

C. Not due to any other physical or mental disorder.

291.80 Alcohol Withdrawal

Differential diagnosis. Alcohol Withdrawal Delirium, Alcohol Hallucinosis, Barbiturate or Similarly Acting Sedative or Hypnotic Withdrawal, hypoglycemia, diabetic ketoacidosis, essential tremor.

Diagnostic criteria.

A. Cessation of or reduction in heavy prolonged (several days or longer) ingestion of alcohol, followed within several hours by coarse tremor of hands, tongue, and eyelids, and at least one of the following:

(1) nausea and vomiting
(2) malaise or weakness
(3) autonomic hyperactivity, e.g., tachycardia,

sweating, elevated blood pressure
(4) anxiety
(5) depressed mood or irritability
(6) orthostatic hypotension

B. Not due to any other physical or mental disorder such as Alcohol Withdrawal Delirium.

291.00 Alcohol Withdrawal Delirium

Differential diagnosis. See Delirium (p. 49).

Diagnostic criteria.

A. Delirium (p. 49) occurs within one week after cessation of or reduction in heavy alcohol ingestion.

B. Autonomic hyperactivity, e.g., tachycardia, sweating, elevated blood pressure.

C. Not due to any other physical or mental disorder.

291.30 Alcohol Hallucinosis

Differential diagnosis. Schizophrenia.

Diagnostic criteria.

A. Organic Hallucinosis (p. 51) with vivid auditory hallucinations developing shortly (usually within 48 hours) after cessation of or reduction in heavy ingestion of alcohol in an individual who apparently has Alcohol Dependence.

B. Response to the hallucinations appropriate to their content, e.g., anxiety in response to hallucinatory threats.

C. No clouding of consciousness, as in Delirium.

D. Not due to any other physical or mental disorder.

291.10 Alcohol Amnestic Disorder

Differential diagnosis. Dementia Associated with Alcoholism. See Amnestic Syndrome, p. 50.

Diagnostic criteria.

A. Amnestic Syndrome (p. 50) following prolonged

heavy ingestion of alcohol.

B. Not due to any other physical or mental disorder.

291.2x Dementia Associated with Alcoholism

Differential diagnosis. Alcohol Amnestic Disorder, Dementia.

Diagnostic criteria.

A. Dementia (p. 49) following prolonged, heavy ingestion of alcohol.

B. Dementia persisting at least three weeks after cessation of alcohol ingestion.

C. Exclusion of all other causes of Dementia, other than prolonged, heavy use of alcohol, by the history, physical examination, and laboratory tests.

Severity criteria.

291.21 Mild: No more than mild impairment in social and occupational functioning.

291.22 Moderate: Moderate social impairment with inability to function occupationally.

291.23 Severe: Severe impairment of functioning with marked deterioration of personality (irritability, social inappropriateness) and inability to function independently.

291.20 Unspecified

Barbiturate or Similarly Acting Sedative or Hypnotic Organic Mental Disorders

305.40 Barbiturate or Similarly Acting Sedative or Hypnotic Intoxication

Differential diagnosis. Intoxication caused by other substances.

Diagnostic criteria.

A. Recent use of a barbiturate or similarly acting sedative or hypnotic.

B. At least one of the following psychological signs:

(1) mood lability
(2) disinhibition of sexual and aggressive impulses
(3) irritability
(4) loquacity

C. At least one of the following neurological signs:

(1) slurred speech
(2) incoordination
(3) unsteady gait
(4) impairment in attention or memory

D. Maladaptive behavioral effects, e.g., impaired judgment, interference with social or occupational functioning, failure to meet responsibilities.

E. Not due to any other physical or mental disorder.

292.00 Barbiturate or Similarly Acting Sedative or Hypnotic Withdrawal

Differential diagnosis. See Alcohol Withdrawal (p. 57).

Diagnostic criteria.

A. Prolonged, heavy use of barbiturate or similarly acting sedative or hypnotic, or more prolonged use of smaller doses of a benzodiazepine.

B. At least three of the following due to recent cessation of or reduction in substance use:

(1) nausea and vomiting
(2) malaise or weakness
(3) autonomic hyperactivity, e.g., tachycardia, sweating, elevated blood pressure
(4) anxiety
(5) depressed mood or irritability
(6) orthostatic hypotension
(7) coarse tremor of hands, tongue, and eyelids

C. Not due to any other physical or mental disorder, such as Barbiturate or Similarly Acting Sedative or Hypnotic Withdrawal Delirium.

292.00 Barbiturate or Similarly Acting Sedative or Hypnotic Withdrawal Delirium

Differential diagnosis. See Alcohol Withdrawal Delirium (p. 58).

Diagnostic criteria.

A. Delirium (p. 49) within one week after cessation of or reduction in heavy use of a barbiturate or similarly acting sedative or hypnotic.

B. Autonomic hyperactivity, e.g., tachycardia, sweating, elevated blood pressure.

C. Not due to any other physical or mental disorder.

292.83 Barbiturate or Similarly Acting Sedative or Hypnotic Amnestic Disorder

Differential diagnosis. See Amnestic Syndrome (p. 50).

Diagnostic criteria.

A. Prolonged, heavy use of a barbiturate or similarly acting sedative or hypnotic.

B. Amnestic Syndrome (p. 50).

C. Not due to any other physical or mental disorder.

Opioid Organic Mental Disorders

305.50 Opioid Intoxication

Differential diagnosis. Other Substance-induced Intoxications, such as Barbiturate and Alcohol Intoxication.

Diagnostic criteria.

A. Recent use of an opioid.

B. Pupillary constriction (or pupillary dilation due to anoxia from severe overdose).

C. At least one of the following psychological signs:

(1) euphoria
(2) dysphoria
(3) apathy
(4) psychomotor retardation

D. At least one of the following neurological signs:

(1) drowsiness
(2) slurred speech
(3) impairment in attention or memory

E. Maladaptive behavioral effects, e.g., impaired judgment, interference with social or occupational functioning.

F. Not due to any other physical or mental disorder.

292.00 Opioid Withdrawal

Differential diagnosis. Influenza; other substance withdrawals especially Barbiturate or Similarly Acting Sedative or Hypnotic Withdrawal.

Diagnostic criteria.

A. Prolonged, heavy use of an opioid (or administration of a narcotic antagonist following a briefer period of use).

B. At least four of the following symptoms due to the recent cessation of or reduction in opioid use:

(1) lacrimation
(2) rhinorrhea
(3) pupillary dilation
(4) piloerection
(5) sweating
(6) diarrhea
(7) yawning
(8) mild hypertension
(9) tachycardia
(10) fever
(11) insomnia

C. Not due to any other physical or mental disorder.

Cocaine Organic Mental Disorder

305.60 Cocaine Intoxication

Differential diagnosis. Manic episode, Amphetamine Intoxication, Phencyclidine (PCP) Intoxication.

Diagnostic criteria.

A. Recent use of cocaine.

B. At least two of the following psychological symptoms:

(1) psychomotor agitation
(2) elation
(3) grandiosity
(4) loquacity
(5) hypervigilance

C. At least two of the following physical symptoms within one hour of using cocaine:

(1) tachycardia
(2) pupillary dilation
(3) elevated blood pressure
(4) perspiration or chills
(5) nausea and vomiting

D. Maladaptive behavioral effects, e.g., fighting, impaired judgment, interference with social or occupational functioning.

E. Not due to any other physical or mental disorder.

Amphetamine or Similarly Acting Sympathomimetic Organic Mental Disorders

305.70 Amphetamine or Similarly Acting Sympathomimetic Intoxication

Differential diagnosis. See Cocaine Intoxication (p. 62).

Diagnostic criteria.

A. Recent use of amphetamine or similarly acting sympathomimetic.

B. Within one hour of use, at least two of the following psychological symptoms:

(1) psychomotor agitation
(2) elation
(3) grandiosity

(4) loquacity
(5) hypervigilance

C. Within one hour of use, at least two of the following physical symptoms:

(1) tachycardia
(2) pupillary dilation
(3) elevated blood pressure
(4) perspiration or chills
(5) nausea or vomiting

D. Maladaptive behavioral effects, e.g., fighting, impaired judgment, interference with social or occupational functioning.

E. Not due to any other physical or mental disorder.

292.81 Amphetamine or Similarly Acting Sympathomimetic Delirium

Differential diagnosis. See Delirium (p. 49).

Diagnostic criteria.

A. Delirium (p. 49) within 24 hours of use of amphetamine or similarly acting sympathomimetic.

B. Not due to any other physical or mental disorder.

292.11 Amphetamine or Similarly Acting Sympathomimetic Delusional Disorder

Differential diagnosis. See Organic Delusional Syndrome, (p. 51).

Diagnostic criteria.

A. Recent use of amphetamine or similarly acting sympathomimetic during a period of long-term use of moderate or high doses.

B. A rapidly developing syndrome consisting of persecutory delusions as the predominant clinical feature and at least three of the following:

(1) ideas of reference
(2) aggressiveness and hostility
(3) anxiety
(4) psychomotor agitation

C. Not due to any other physical or mental disorder.

292.00 Amphetamine or Similarly Acting Sympathomimetic Withdrawal

Differential diagnosis. Depressive Disorder.

Diagnostic criteria.

A. Prolonged heavy use of amphetamine or a similarly acting sympathomimetic.

B. After cessation of or reduction in substance use, depressed mood and at least two of the following:

(1) fatigue
(2) disturbed sleep
(3) increased dreaming

C. Not due to any other physical or mental disorder, such as Amphetamine or Similarly Acting Sympathomimetic Delusional Disorder.

Phencyclidine (PCP) or Similarly Acting Arylcyclohexylamine Organic Mental Disorders

305.90 Phencyclidine or Similarly Acting Arylcyclohexylamine Intoxication

Differential diagnosis. Other substance-induced intoxications.

Diagnostic criteria.

A. Recent use of phencyclidine or a similarly acting arylcyclohexylamine.

B. Within an hour (less when smoked, insufflated, or used intravenously), at least two of the following physical symptoms:

(1) vertical or horizontal nystagmus
(2) increased blood pressure and heart rate
(3) numbness or diminished responsiveness to pain
(4) ataxia
(5) dysarthria

C. Within one hour, at least two of the following psychological symptoms:

(1) euphoria
(2) psychomotor agitation
(3) marked anxiety

(4) emotional lability
(5) grandiosity
(6) sensation of slowed time
(7) synesthesias

D. Maladaptive behavioral effects, e.g., belligerence, impulsivity, unpredictability, impaired judgment, assaultiveness.

E. Not due to any other physical or mental disorder, e.g., Delirium.

292.81 Phencyclidine (PCP) or Similarly Acting Arylcyclohexylamine Delirium

Differential diagnosis. See Delirium (p. 49).

Diagnostic criteria.

A. Delirium (p. 49) due to phencyclidine (PCP) or similarly acting arylcyclohexylamine.

B. Not due to any other physical or mental disorder.

292.90 Phencyclidine (PCP) or Similarly Acting Arylcyclohexylamine Mixed Organic Mental Disorder

Diagnostic criteria.

A. There is evidence of recent use of phencyclidine or a similarly acting arylcyclohexylamine.

B. The resulting illness involves features of several organic brain syndromes or a progression from one organic brain syndrome to another, e.g., initially there is Delirium, followed by an Organic Delusional Syndrome.

Hallucinogen Organic Mental Disorders

305.30 Hallucinogen Hallucinosis

Differential diagnosis. Other substance-induced intoxications, see Organic Hallucinosis (p. 51).

Diagnostic criteria.

A. Recent ingestion of a hallucinogen.

B. Perceptual changes occurring in a state of full

wakefulness and alertness, e.g., subjective intensification of perceptions, depersonalization, derealization, illusions, hallucinations, synesthesias.

C. At least two of the following physical symptoms:

(1) pupillary dilation
(2) tachycardia
(3) sweating
(4) palpitations
(5) blurring of vision
(6) tremors
(7) incoordination

D. Maladaptive behavioral effects, e.g., marked anxiety or depression, ideas of reference, fear of losing one's mind, paranoid ideation, impaired judgment, interference with social or occupational functioning.

E. Not due to any other physical or mental disorder.

292.11 Hallucinogen Delusional Disorder

Differential diagnosis. Pre-existing nonorganic psychotic disorder, see Organic Delusional Syndrome (p. 51).

Diagnostic criteria.

A. Recent hallucinogen use.

B. Development of an Organic Delusional Syndrome (p. 51) that persists beyond 24 hours after cessation of hallucinogen use.

C. Not due to any other physical or mental disorder, such as Schizophrenia.

292.84 Hallucinogen Affective Disorder

Differential diagnosis. Pre-existing Affective Disorder; Hallucinogen Delusional Disorder, see Organic Affective Syndrome (p. 52).

Diagnostic criteria.

A. Recent hallucinogen use.

B. Development of an Organic Affective Syndrome (p. 52) that persists beyond 24 hours after cessation of hallucinogen use.

C. Absence of delusions.

D. Not due to any other physical or mental disorder, such as pre-existing Affective Disorder.

Cannabis Organic Mental Disorders

305.20 Cannabis Intoxication

Differential diagnosis. Other substance-induced intoxications.

Diagnostic criteria.

A. Recent use of cannabis.

B. Tachycardia.

C. At least one of the following psychological symptoms within 2 hours of use:

(1) euphoria
(2) subjective intensification of perceptions
(3) sensation of slowed time
(4) apathy

D. At least one of the following physical symptoms within 2 hours of substance use:

(1) conjunctival injection
(2) increased appetite
(3) dry mouth

E. Maladaptive behavioral effects, e.g., excessive anxiety, suspiciousness or paranoid ideation, impaired judgment, interference with social or occupational functioning.

292.11 Cannabis Delusional Disorder

Differential diagnosis. See Organic Delusional Syndrome (p. 51).

Diagnostic criteria.

A. Recent use of cannabis.

B. An Organic Delusional Syndrome (p. 62) within 2 hours of substance use.

C. The disturbance does not persist beyond six hours following cessation of substance use.

D. Not due to any other physical or mental disorder.

Tobacco Organic Mental Disorder

292.00 Tobacco Withdrawal

Diagnostic criteria.

A. Use of tobacco for at least several weeks at a level equivalent to more than ten cigarettes per day, with each cigarette containing at least 0.5 mg of nicotine.

B. Abrupt cessation of or reduction in tobacco use, followed within 24 hours by at least four of the following:

(1) craving for tobacco
(2) irritability
(3) anxiety
(4) difficulty concentrating
(5) restlessness
(6) headache
(7) drowsiness
(8) gastrointestinal disturbances

Caffeine Organic Mental Disorder

305.90 Caffeine Intoxication

Differential diagnosis. Manic episode, Panic Disorder, Generalized Anxiety Disorder.

Diagnostic criteria.

A. Recent consumption of caffeine, usually in excess of 250 mg.

B. At least five of the following:

(1) restlessness
(2) nervousness
(3) excitement
(4) insomnia
(5) flushed face
(6) diuresis
(7) gastrointestinal complaints
(8) muscle twitching
(9) rambling flow of thought and speech
(10) cardiac arrhythmia
(11) periods of inexhaustibility
(12) psychomotor agitation

C. Not due to any other mental disorder, such as an Anxiety Disorder.

Other or Unspecified Substance-induced Mental Disorders

This section is to be used when an individual develops an Organic Brain Syndrome apparently due to use of a substance if:

(1) the substance cannot be classified in any of the ten previously listed categories (examples: Levo-dopa Delusional Disorder, Anticholinergic Delirium);
(2) the syndrome is caused by an unknown substance (example: an intoxication after taking a bottle of unlabeled pills).

Following the listing of each of the diagnoses in this section, the reader is directed to the page listing the diagnostic criteria for the various Organic Brain Syndromes.

292.81 Other or Unspecified Substance Delirium **(p. 49)**

292.82 Other or Unspecified Substance Dementia **(p. 49)**

292.83 Other or Unspecified Substance Amnestic Disorder **(p. 50)**

292.11 Other or Unspecified Substance Delusional Disorder (p. 51)

292.12 Other or Unspecified Substance Hallucinosis (p. 51)

292.84 Other or Unspecified Substance Affective Disorder (p. 52)

292.89 Other or Unspecified Substance Personality Disorder (p. 52)

305.90 Other or Unspecified Substance Intoxication (p. 53)

292.00 Other or Unspecified Substance Withdrawal (p. 54)

292.90 Other or Unspecified Substance Atypical or Mixed Organic Mental Disorder (p. 54)

SECTION 2. Organic Mental Disorders in which the etiology or pathophysiological process is either noted as an additional diagnosis from outside of the mental disorders section of ICD-9-CM (Axis III) or is unknown.

This section permits the identification of specific Organic Brain Syndromes on Axis I associated with physical disorders noted on Axis III. Examples would include Delirium (Axis I) associated with pneumonia (Axis III) and Dementia (Axis I) associated with brain tumor (Axis III). Following the name of each of the Organic Brain Syndromes is the page listing the diagnostic criteria for the syndrome.

293.00 Delirium (p. 49)

294.10 Dementia (p. 49)

294.00 Amnestic Syndrome (p. 50)

293.81 Organic Delusional Syndrome (p. 51)

293.82 Organic Hallucinosis (p. 51)

293.83 Organic Affective Syndrome (p. 52)

310.10 Organic Personality Syndrome (p. 52)

294.80 Atypical or Mixed Organic Brain Syndrome (p. 54)

Subclassification of Course. For each Substance Use Disorder, the course of illness is noted in the fifth digit using the following guidelines:

Code	Course	Definition
1	Continuous	More or less regular maladaptive use for over six months.
2	Episodic	A fairly circumscribed period of maladaptive use, with one or more similar periods in the past.
3	In Remission	Previous maladaptive use, but not using substances at present. The differentiation of this from no longer ill and from the other course categories requires consideration of the period of time since the last period of disturbance, the total duration of the disturbance, and the need for continued evaluation or prophylactic treatment.
0	Unspecified	Course unknown or first signs of illness with course uncertain.

305.0x Alcohol Abuse

Differential diagnosis. Nonpathological recreational use of a substance, episodes of intoxication without a pattern of pathological use.

Diagnostic criteria.

A. *Pattern of pathological alcohol use:* need for daily use of alcohol for adequate functioning; inability to cut down or stop drinking; repeated efforts to control or reduce excess drinking by "going on the wagon" (periods of temporary abstinence) or restricting drinking to certain times of the day; binges (remaining intoxicated throughout the day for at least two days); occasional consumption of a fifth of spirits (or its equivalent in wine or beer); amnesic periods for events occurring while intoxicated (blackouts); continuation of drinking despite a serious physical disorder that the individual knows is exacerbated by alcohol use; drinking of nonbeverage alcohol.

B. *Impairment in social or occupational functioning due to alcohol use:* e.g., violence while intoxicated, absence from work, loss of job, legal difficulties (e.g., arrest for intoxicated behavior, traffic accidents while intoxicated), arguments or difficulties with family or friends because of excessive alcohol use.

C. Duration of disturbance of at least one month.

303.9x Alcohol Dependence

Diagnostic criteria.

A. Either a pattern of pathological use or impairment in social or occupational functioning due to alcohol use.

Pattern of pathological alcohol use: daily use of alcohol is a prerequisite for adequate functioning; inability to cut down or stop drinking; repeated efforts to control or reduce excess drinking by "going on the wagon" (periods of temporary abstinence) or restriction of drinking to certain times of the day; drinks non-beverage alcohol; goes on binges (remains intoxicated throughout the day for at least two days); occasionally drinks a fifth of spirits (or its equivalent in wine or beer); has had two or more "blackouts" (amnesic period for events occurring while intoxicated); continues to drink despite a serious physical disorder that the individual knows is exacerbated by alcohol use.

Impairment in social or occupational functioning due to alcohol use: e.g., violence while intoxicated, absence from work, loss of job, legal difficulties (e.g., arrest for intoxicated behavior, traffic accidents while intoxicated), arguments or difficulties with family or friends because of excessive alcohol use.

B. Either tolerance or withdrawal:

(1) *Tolerance:* need for markedly increased amounts of alcohol to achieve the desired effect, or markedly diminished effect with regular use of the same amount.

(2) *Withdrawal:* development of Alcohol Withdrawal (e.g., morning "shakes" and malaise relieved by drinking) after cessation of or reduction in drinking (p. 57).

305.4x Barbiturate or Similarly Acting Sedative or Hypnotic Abuse

Diagnostic criteria.

A. *Pattern of pathological use:* inability to cut down or stop use; intoxication throughout the day; frequent use of the equivalent of 600 mg or more of secobarbital or 60 mg or more of diazepam; amnesic periods for events that occurred while intoxicated.

B. *Impairment in social or occupational functioning due to substance use:* e.g., fights, loss of friends, absence from work, loss of job, or legal difficulties (other than a single arrest due to possession, purchase or sale of the substance).

C. Duration of disturbance of at least one month.

304.1x Barbiturate or Similarly Acting Sedative or Hypnotic Dependence

Diagnostic criteria.

Either tolerance or withdrawal:

Tolerance: need for markedly increased amounts of

the substance to achieve the desired effect, or markedly diminished effect with regular use of the same amount.

Withdrawal: development of Barbiturate or Similarly Acting Sedative or Hypnotic Withdrawal (p. 60) after cessation of or reduction in substance use.

305.5x Opioid Abuse

Diagnostic criteria.

A. *Pattern of pathological use:* inability to reduce or stop use; intoxication throughout the day; use of opioids nearly every day for at least a month; episodes of opioid overdose (intoxication so severe that respiration and consciousness are impaired).

B. *Impairment in social or occupational functioning due to opioid use:* e.g., fights, loss of friends, absence from work, loss of job, or legal difficulties (other than due to a single arrest for possession, purchase, or sale of the substance).

C. Duration of disturbance of at least one month.

304.0x Opioid Dependence

Diagnostic criteria.

Either tolerance or withdrawal:

Tolerance: need for markedly increased amounts of opioid to achieve the desired effect, or markedly diminished effect with regular use of the same amount.

Withdrawal: development of Opioid Withdrawal (p. 62) after cessation of or reduction in substance use.

305.6x Cocaine Abuse

Diagnostic criteria.

A. *Pattern of pathological use:* inability to reduce or stop use; intoxication throughout the day; episodes of cocaine overdose (intoxication so severe that hallucinations and delusions occur in a clear sensorium).

B. *Impairment in social or occupational functioning due to cocaine use*: e.g., fights, loss of friends, absence from work, loss of job, or legal difficulties (other than due to a single arrest for possession, purchase, or sale of the substance).

C. Duration of disturbance of at least one month.

305.7x Amphetamine or Similarly Acting Sympathomimetic Abuse

Diagnostic criteria.

A. *Pattern of pathological use:* inability to reduce or stop use; intoxication throughout the day; use of substance nearly every day for at least one month; episodes of either Amphetamine or Similarly Acting Sympathomimetic Delusional Disorder or Amphetamine or Similarly Acting Sympathomimetic Delirium.

B. *Impairment in social or occupational functioning due to amphetamine or similarly acting sympathomimetic use:* e.g., fights, loss of friends, absence from work, loss of job, or legal difficulties (other than due to a single arrest for possession, purchase, or sale of the substance).

C. Duration of disturbance of at least one month.

304.4x Amphetamine or Similarly Acting Sympathomimetic Dependence

Diagnostic criteria.

Either tolerance or withdrawal:

Tolerance: need for markedly increased amounts of the substance to achieve the desired effect or markedly diminished effect with regular use of the same amount.

Withdrawal: development of Amphetamine or Similarly Acting Sympathomimetic Withdrawal (p. 65) after cessation of or reduction in substance use.

305.9x Phencyclidine (PCP) or Similarly Acting Arylcyclohexylamine Abuse

Diagnostic criteria.

A. *Pattern of pathological use:* intoxication throughout the day; episodes of Phencyclidine or Similarly Acting Arylcyclohexylamine Delirium or Mixed Organic Mental Disorder.

B. *Impairment in social or occupational functioning due to substance use:* e.g., fights, loss of friends, absence from work, loss of job, or legal difficulties (other than due to a single arrest for possession, purchase, or sale of the substance).

C. Duration of disturbance of at least one month.

305.3x Hallucinogen Abuse

Diagnostic criteria.

A. *Pattern of pathological use:* inability to reduce or stop use; intoxication throughout the day (possible only with some hallucinogens); episodes of Hallucinogen Delusional Disorder.

B. *Impairment in social or occupational functioning due to hallucinogen use:* e.g., fights, loss of friends, absence from work, loss of job, or legal difficulties (other than due to a single arrest for possession, purchase, or sale of the substance).

C. Duration of disturbance of at least one month.

305.2x Cannabis Abuse

Diagnostic criteria.

A. *Pattern of pathological use:* intoxication throughout the day; use of cannabis nearly every day for at least one month; episodes of Cannabis Delusional Disorder.

B. *Impairment in social or occupational functioning due to cannabis use:* e.g. marked loss of interest in activities previously engaged in, loss of friends, absence from work, loss of job, or legal difficulties (other than a single arrest due to possession, purchase, or sale of the substance).

304.3x Cannabis Dependence

Diagnostic criteria.

A. Either a pattern of pathological use or impairment in social or occupational functioning due to cannabis use.

Pattern of pathological use: inability to reduce or stop use; repeated efforts to control use with periods of temporary abstinence or restriction of use to certain times of the day; is intoxicated throughout the day; uses cannabis nearly every day for at least one month; has had two or more episodes of Cannabis Delusional Disorder.

Impairment in social or occupational functioning due to cannabis use: e.g., marked loss of interest in activities previously engaged in, loss of friends, absence from work, loss of job, or legal difficulties (other than due to a single arrest for possession, purchase, or sale of an illegal substance).

B. *Tolerance:* need for markedly increased amounts of cannabis to achieve the desired effect or markedly diminished effect with regular use of the same amount.

305.1x Tobacco Dependence

Diagnostic criteria.

A. Continuous use of tobacco for at least one month.

B. At least one of the following:

(1) serious attempts to stop or significantly reduce the amount of tobacco use on a permanent basis have been unsuccessful
(2) attempts to stop smoking have led to the development of Tobacco Withdrawal (see p. 69)
(3) the individual continues to use tobacco despite a serious physical disorder (e.g., respiratory or cardiovascular disease) that he or she knows is exacerbated by tobacco use

305.9x Other, Mixed, or Unspecified Substance Abuse

Other Substance Abuse should be recorded if a substance abused cannot be classified in any of the categories noted above, e.g., glue (inhalants), amyl nitrite.

Mixed Substance Abuse should be noted when the substances abused are from more than one nonalcoholic substance category, e.g., amphetamines and barbiturates. This category should be used only when the specific substances cannot be identified or when the abuse involves so many substances that the clinician prefers to indicate a combination of substances rather than list each specific substance.

Unspecified Substance Abuse should be recorded when a substance abused is unknown.

304.6x Other Specified Substance Dependence

This category should be used when the individual is dependent on a substance that cannot be classified in any of the previous categories, e.g., codeine or corticosteroids.

304.9x Unspecified Substance Dependence

This diagnosis can be used as an initial diagnosis in cases in which the specific substance is not yet known.

304.7x Dependence on Combination of Opioid and Other Nonalcoholic Substance

This category should be used when the individual is dependent on both an opioid and a nonopioid nonalcoholic substance. An example might be dependence on both heroin and barbiturates. This category should be used only when the specific substances cannot be identified or when the dependence involves so many substances that the clinician prefers to indicate a combination of substances rather than list each specific substance.

304.8x Dependence on a Combination of Substances, Excluding Opioids and Alcohol

This category should be used when the individual is dependent on two or more nonopioid nonalcoholic substances. An example might be dependence on both amphetamines and barbiturates. This category should be used only when the specific substances cannot be identified or when the dependence involves so many substances that the clinician prefers to indicate a combination of substances rather than list each specific substance.

Differential diagnosis. Organic Mental Disorders, such as Organic Delusional Syndromes due to amphetamines or phencyclidine; Mental Retardation; Paranoid Disorders; major depressive and manic episodes with psychotic features; Schizoaffective Disorder; Schizophreniform Disorder; Pervasive Developmental Disorder; overvalued ideas in Obsessive Compulsive Disorder, Hypochondriasis, and Phobic Disorder; Factitious Disorder with Psychological Symptoms; transient psychotic symptoms in Schizotypal, Histrionic, Nacissistic, Borderline, and Paranoid Personality Disorders; odd beliefs or experiences of members of religious or other subcultural groups.

Diagnostic criteria.

A. At least one of the following during a phase of the illness:

(1) bizarre delusions (content is patently absurd and has *no* possible basis in fact), such as delusions of being controlled, thought broadcasting, thought insertion, or thought withdrawal
(2) somatic, grandiose, religious, nihilistic, or other delusions without persecutory or jealous content
(3) delusions with persecutory or jealous content if accompanied by hallucinations of any type
(4) auditory hallucinations in which either a voice keeps up a running commentary on the individual's behavior or thoughts or two or more voices converse with each other
(5) auditory hallucinations on several occasions with content of more than one or two words having no apparent relation to depression or elation
(6) incoherence, marked loosening of associations, markedly illogical thinking, or marked poverty of content of speech if associated with at least one of the following:

(*a*) blunted, flat, or inappropriate affect
(*b*) delusions or hallucinations
(*c*) catatonic or other grossly disorganized behavior

B. Deterioration from a previous level of functioning in such areas as work, social relations, and self-care.

C. Duration: Continuous signs of the illness for at least six months at some time during the person's life with some signs of the illness at present. The six-month period must include an active phase during which there were symptoms from A, with or without a prodromal or residual phase, as defined below.

Prodromal phase: A clear deterioration in functioning before the active phase of the illness not due to a disturbance in mood or to a Substance Use Disorder and involving at least *two* of the symptoms noted below.

Residual phase: Persistence following the active phase of the illness, of at least *two* of the symptoms noted below not due to a disturbance in mood or to a Substance Use Disorder.

Prodromal or Residual Symptoms

(1) social isolation or withdrawal

(2) marked impairment in role functioning as wage-earner, student, or homemaker

(3) markedly peculiar behavior (e.g., collecting garbage, talking to self in public, hoarding food)

(4) marked impairment in personal hygiene and grooming

(5) blunted, flat, or inappropriate affect

(6) digressive, vague, overelaborate, circumstantial, or metaphorical speech

(7) odd or bizarre ideation, or magical thinking, e.g., superstitiousness, clairvoyance, telepathy, "sixth sense," "others can feel my feelings," overvalued ideas, ideas of reference

(8) unusual perceptual experiences, e.g., recurrent illusions, sensing the presence of a force or person not actually present

Examples: Six months of prodromal symptoms with one week of symptoms from A; no prodromal symptoms with six months of symptoms from A; no prodromal symptoms with two weeks of symptoms from A and six months of residual symptoms; six months of symptoms from A, apparently followed by several years of complete remission, with one week of symptoms in A in current episode.

D. The full depressive or manic syndrome (criteria A and B of major depressive or manic episode), if present, developed after any psychotic symptoms, or was brief in duration relative to the duration of the psychotic symptoms in A.

E. Onset of prodromal or active phase of the illness before age 45.

F. Not due to any Organic Mental Disorder or Mental Retardation.

TYPES

The diagnosis of a particular type should be based on the predominant clinical picture that occasioned the evaluation or admission to clinical care.

295.1x Disorganized Type

Diagnostic criteria.

A type of Schizophrenia in which there are:

A. Frequent incoherence.

B. Absence of systematized delusions.

C. Blunted, inappropriate, or silly affect.

295.2x Catatonic Type

Diagnostic criteria.

A type of Schizophrenia dominated by any of the following:

(1) catatonic stupor (marked decrease in reactivity to environment and/or reduction of spontaneous movements and activity) or mutism

(2) catatonic negativism (an apparently motiveless resistance to all instructions or attempts to be moved)

(3) catatonic rigidity (maintenance of a rigid posture against efforts to be moved)

(4) catatonic excitement (excited motor activity, apparently purposeless and not influenced by external stimuli)

(5) catatonic posturing (voluntary assumption of inappropriate or bizarre posture)

295.3x Paranoid Type

Diagnostic criteria.

A type of Schizophrenia dominated by any of the following:

(1) persecutory delusions
(2) grandiose delusions
(3) delusional jealousy
(4) hallucinations with persecutory or grandiose content

295.9x Undifferentiated Type

Diagnostic criteria.

A type of Schizophrenia in which there are:

A. Prominent delusions, hallucinations, incoherence, or grossly disorganized behavior.

B. Does not meet the criteria for any of the previously listed types or meets the criteria for more than one.

295.6x Residual Type

Diagnostic criteria.

A type of Schizophrenia in which there are:

A. A history of at least one previous episode of Schizophrenia with prominent psychotic symptoms.

B. A clinical picture without any prominent psychotic symptoms that occasioned evaluation or admission to clinical care.

C. Continuing evidence of the illness, such as blunted or inappropriate affect, social withdrawal, eccentric behavior, illogical thinking, or loosening of associations.

CLASSIFICATION OF COURSE

The course of the illness is coded in the fifth digit:

(1) *Subchronic.* The time from the beginning of the illness, during which the individual began to show signs of the illness (including prodromal, active, and residual phases) more or less continuously, is less than two years but at least six months.

(2) *Chronic.* Same as above, but greater than two years.

(3) *Subchronic with Acute Exacerbation.* Reemergence of prominent psychotic symptoms in an individual with a subchronic course who has been in the residual phase of the illness.

(4) *Chronic with Acute Exacerbation.* Reemergence of prominent psychotic symptoms in an individual with a chronic course who has been in the residual phase of the illness.

(5) *In Remission.* This should be used when an individual with a history of Schizophrenia, now is free of all signs of the illness (whether or not on medication). The differentiation of Schizophrenia In Remission from no mental disorder requires consideration of the period of time since the last episode, the number of episodes, and the need for continued evaluation of prophylactic treatment.

When the course is noted as "In Remission," the phenomenologic type should describe the last episode of Schizophrenia, e.g., 295.25 Schizophrenia, Catatonic Type, In Remission.
When the phenomenology of the last episode is unknown, it should be noted as Undifferentiated.

Paranoid Disorders

Paranoid Disorder

Differential diagnosis. Organic Delusional Syndromes, particularly those induced by amphetamines; Schizophrenia, Paranoid Type; Schizophreniform Disorder; Paranoid Personality Disorder.

Diagnostic criteria.

A. Persistent persecutory delusions or delusional jealousy.

B. Emotion and behavior appropriate to the content of the delusional system.

C. Duration of illness of at least one week.

D. None of the symptoms of criterion A of Schizophrenia (p. 83), such as bizarre delusions, incoherence, or marked loosening of associations.

E. No prominent hallucinations.

F. The full depressive or manic syndrome (criteria A and B of major depressive or manic episode, p. 95 and p. 97) is either not present, developed after any psychotic symptoms, or was brief in duration relative to the duration of the psychotic symptoms.

G. Not due to an Organic Mental Disorder.

297.10 Paranoia

Diagnostic criteria.

A. Meets the criteria for Paranoid Disorder (above).

B. A chronic and stable persecutory delusional system of at least six months' duration.

C. Does not meet the criteria for Shared Paranoid Disorder (below).

297.30 Shared Paranoid Disorder

Diagnostic criteria.

A. Meets the criteria for Paranoid Disorder.

B. Delusional system develops as a result of a close friendship with another person or persons who have an established paranoid psychotic disorder.

298.30 Acute Paranoid Disorder

Diagnostic criteria.

A. Meets the criteria for Paranoid Disorder (p. 89).

B. Duration of less than six months.

C. Does not meet the criteria for Shared Paranoid Disorder (above).

297.90 Atypical Paranoid Disorder

This is a residual category for Paranoid Disorders not classified in any of the specific categories.

Psychotic Disorders Not Elsewhere Classified

295.40 Schizophreniform Disorder

Differential diagnosis. Schizophrenia, Brief Reactive Psychosis.

Diagnostic criteria.

A. Meets all of the criteria for Schizophrenia (p. 103) except for duration.

B. The illness (including prodromal, active, and residual phases) lasts more than two weeks but less than six months.

298.80 Brief Reactive Psychosis

Differential diagnosis. Schizophreniform Disorder; Paranoid Disorder; major depressive and manic episodes with psychotic features; Organic Mental Disorders, particularly Delirium, Organic Delusional Syndrome, and Intoxication; transient psychotic symptoms in Personality Disorders; Factitious Disorder with Psychological Symptoms; Malingering.

Diagnostic criteria.

A. Psychotic symptoms appear immediately following a recognizable psychosocial stressor that would evoke significant symptoms of distress in almost anyone.

B. The clinical picture involves emotional turmoil and at least one of the following psychotic symptoms:

(1) incoherence or loosening of associations
(2) delusions
(3) hallucinations
(4) behavior that is grossly disorganized or catatonic

C. The psychotic symptoms last more than a few

hours but less than two weeks, and there is an eventual return to the premorbid level of functioning. (Note: The diagnosis can be made soon after the onset of the psychotic symptoms without waiting for the expected recovery. If the psychotic symptoms last more than two weeks, the diagnosis should be changed.)

D. No period of increasing psychopathology immediately preceded the psychosocial stressor.

E. Not due to any other mental disorder, such as an Organic Mental Disorder, manic episode, or Factitious Disorder with Psychological Symptoms.

295.70 Schizoaffective Disorder

This category is retained in this manual without diagnostic criteria for those instances in which the clinician is unable to make a differential diagnosis with any degree of certainty between Affective Disorder and either Schizophreniform Disorder or Schizophrenia. Before using the Schizoaffective Disorder category, the clinician should consider the following diagnoses: Schizophreniform Disorder, Major Depression or Bipolar Disorder With Psychotic Features, and Schizophrenia with a superimposed Atypical Affective Disorder.

Examples of cases that may appropriately be diagnosed as Schizoaffective Disorder include:

An episode of affective illness in which preoccupation with a mood-incongruent delusion or hallucination dominates the clinical picture when affective symptoms are no longer present.

An episode of illness in which currently there is a full affective syndrome with prominent mood-incongruent psychotic features but in which inadequate information about the presence of previous nonaffective psychotic features make it difficult to differentiate between Schizophrenia or Schizophreniform Disorder (with a superimposed Atypical Affective Disorder) and Affective Disorder.

298.90 Atypical Psychosis

This is a residual category for cases in which there are psychotic symptoms (delusions, hallucinations, incoherence, loosening of associations, marked poverty of content of thought, markedly illogical thinking, or behavior that is grossly disorganized or catatonic) that do not meet the criteria for any specific mental disorder.

Common examples of this category include:

(1) Psychoses with unusual features, e.g., monosymptomatic delusion of bodily change without accompanying impairment in functioning; persistent auditory hallucinations as the only disturbance; transient psychotic episodes associated with the menstrual cycle.

(2) "Postpartum Psychoses" that do not meet the criteria for an Organic Mental Disorder, Schizophreniform Disorder, Paranoid Disorder, or Affective Disorder.

(3) Psychoses that would be classified elsewhere except that the duration is less than two weeks, e.g., the symptomatology of a Schizophreniform Disorder, but lasting only three days.

(4) Psychoses about which there is inadequate information to make a more specific diagnosis. (This is preferable to Diagnosis Deferred, and can be changed if more information becomes available.)

(5) Psychoses with confusing clinical features that make a more specific diagnosis impossible.

MAJOR AFFECTIVE DISORDERS

Manic Episode

Differential diagnosis. Organic Affective Syndromes; Schizophrenia, Paranoid Type; Schizoaffective Disorder; Cyclothymic Disorder.

Diagnostic criteria.

A. One or more distinct periods with a predominantly elevated, expansive, or irritable mood. The elevated or irritable mood must be a prominent part of the illness and relatively persistent, although it may alternate or intermingle with depressive mood.

B. Duration of at least one week (or any duration if hospitalization is necessary), during which, for most of the time, at least three of the following symptoms have persisted (four if the mood is only irritable) and have been present to a significant degree:

(1) increase in activity (either socially, at work, or sexually) or physical restlessness
(2) more talkative than usual or pressure to keep talking
(3) flight of ideas or subjective experience that thoughts are racing
(4) inflated self-esteem (grandiosity, which may be delusional)
(5) decreased need for sleep
(6) distractibility, i.e., attention too easily drawn to unimportant or irrelevant external stimuli
(7) excessive involvement in activities that have a high potential for painful consequences which is not recognized, e.g., buying sprees, sexual indiscretions, foolish business investments, reckless driving

C. Neither of the following dominate the clinical picture when an affective syndrome (i.e., criteria A and B above) is not present, that is, before it developed or after it has remitted:

(1) preoccupation with a mood-incongruent delusion or hallucination (see definition below)
(2) bizarre behavior

D. Not superimposed on either Schizophrenia, Schizophreniform Disorder, or a Paranoid Disorder.

E. Not due to any Organic Mental Disorder, such as Substance Intoxication.

(*Note:* A hypomanic episode is a pathological disturbance similar to, but not as severe as, a manic episode. See Atypical Bipolar Disorder, p. 104.)

Fifth-digit code numbers and criteria for subclassification of manic episode:

6–**In Remission.** This fifth-digit category should be used when in the past the individual met the full criteria for a manic episode but now is essentially free of manic symptoms or has some signs of the disorder but does not meet the full criteria. The differentiation of this diagnosis from no mental disorder requires consideration of the period of time since the last episode, the number of previous episodes, and the need for continued evaluation or prophylactic treatment.

4–**With Psychotic Features.** This fifth-digit category should be used when there apparently is gross impairment in reality testing, as when there are delusions or hallucinations or grossly bizarre behavior. When possible specify whether the psychotic features are mood-congruent or mood-incongruent. (The non-ICD-9-CM fifth-digit 7 may be used instead to indicate that the psychotic features are mood-incongruent; otherwise, mood-congruence may be assumed.)

Mood-congruent Psychotic Features: Delusions or hallucinations whose content is entirely consistent with the themes of inflated worth, power, knowledge, identity, or special relationship to a deity or famous person; flight of ideas without apparent awareness by the individual that the speech is not understandable.

Mood-incongruent Psychotic Features: Either (*a*) or (*b*):

(*a*) Delusions or hallucinations whose content does not involve themes of either inflated worth, power, knowledge, identity, or special relationship to a deity or famous person. Included are such symptoms as persecutory delusions, thought insertion, and delusions of being controlled, whose content has no apparent relationship to any of the themes noted above.

(*b*) Any of the following catatonic symptoms: stupor, mutism, negativism, posturing.

2–**Without Psychotic Features.** Meets the criteria for manic episode, but no psychotic features are present.

0–**Unspecified.**

Major depressive episode

Differential diagnosis. Organic Affective Syndrome, Primary Degenerative Dementia, Multi-infarct Dementia, psychological reaction to functional impairment associated with a physical illness, Schizophrenia, Schizoaffective Disorder, Dysthymic Disorder, Cyclothymic Disorder, other chronic mental disorders associated with depressive symptoms, Separation Anxiety Disorder, Uncomplicated Bereavement.

Diagnostic criteria.

A. Dysphoric mood or loss of interest or pleasure in all or almost all usual activities and pastimes. The dysphoric mood is characterized by symptoms such as the following: depressed, sad, blue, hopeless, low, down in the dumps, irritable. The mood disturbance must be prominent and relatively persistent, but not necessarily the most dominant symptom, and does not include momentary shifts from one dysphoric mood to another dysphoric mood, e.g., anxiety to depression to anger, such as are seen in states of acute psychotic turmoil. (For children under six, dysphoric mood may have to be inferred from a persistently sad facial expression.)

B. At least four of the following symptoms have each been present nearly every day for a period of at least two weeks (in children under six, at least three of the first four):

(1) poor appetite or significant weight loss (when not dieting) or increased appetite or significant weight gain (in children under six consider failure to make expected weight gains)
(2) insomnia or hypersomnia
(3) psychomotor agitation or retardation (but not merely subjective feelings of restlessness or being slowed down) (in children under six, hypoactivity)
(4) loss of interest or pleasure in usual activities, or decrease in sexual drive not limited to a period when delusional or hallucinating (in children under six, signs of apathy)
(5) loss of energy; fatigue
(6) feelings of worthlessness, self-reproach, or excessive or inappropriate guilt (either may be delusional)
(7) complaints or evidence of diminished ability to think or concentrate, such as slowed thinking, or indecisiveness not associated with marked loosening of associations or incoherence
(8) recurrent thoughts of death, suicidal ideation, wishes to be dead, or suicide attempt

C. Neither of the following dominate the clinical picture when an affectve syndrome (i.e., criteria A and B above) is not present, that is, before it developed or after it has remitted:

(1) preoccupation with a mood-incongruent delusion or hallucination (see definition below)
(2) bizarre behavior

D. Not superimposed on either Schizophrenia, Schizophreniform Disorder, or a Paranoid Disorder.

E. Not due to any Organic Mental Disorder or Uncomplicated Bereavement.

Fifth-digit code numbers and criteria for subclassification of major depressive episode:

(When psychotic features and melancholia are present the coding system requires that the clinician record the single most clinically significant characteristic.)

6–**In Remission.** This fifth-digit category should be used when in the past the individual met the full criteria for a major depressive episode but now is essentially free of depressive symptoms or has some signs of the disorder but does not meet the full criteria.

4–**With Psychotic Features.** This fifth-digit category should be used when there apparently is gross impairment in reality testing, as when there are delusions or hallucinations, or depressive stupor (the individual is mute and unresponsive). When possible specify whether the psychotic features are mood-congruent or mood-incongruent. (The non-ICD-9-CM fifth-digit 7 may be used instead to indicate that the psychotic features are mood-incongruent; otherwise, mood-congruence may be assumed.)

Mood-congruent Psychotic Features. Delusions or hallucinations whose content is entirely consistent with the themes of either personal inadequacy, guilt, disease, death, nihilism, or deserved punishment; depressive stupor (the individual is mute and unresponsive).

Mood-incongruent Psychotic Features. Delusions or hallucinations whose content does not involve themes of either personal inadequacy, guilt, disease, death, nihilism, or deserved punishment. Included here are such symptoms as persecutory delusions, thought insertion, thought broadcasting, and delusions of control, whose content has no apparent relationship to any of the themes noted above.

3–With Melancholia.

A. Loss of pleasure in all or almost all activities.

B. Lack of reactivity to usually pleasurable stimuli (doesn't feel much better, even temporarily, when something good happens).

C. At least three of the following:

(a) distinct quality of depressed mood, i.e., the

depressed mood is perceived as distinctly different from the kind of feeling experienced following the death of a loved one
(*b*) the depression is regularly worse in the morning
(*c*) early morning awakening (at least two hours before usual time of awakening)
(*d*) marked psychomotor retardation or agitation
(*e*) significant anorexia or weight loss
(*f*) excessive or inappropriate guilt

2–**Without Melancholia**

0–**Unspecified**

BIPOLAR DISORDER

296.6x Bipolar Disorder, Mixed

Diagnostic criteria.

Use fifth-digit coding for manic episode.

A. Current (or most recent) episode involves the full symptomatic picture of both manic and major depressive episodes (p. 95 and p. 97), intermixed or rapidly alternating every few days.

B. Depressive symptoms are prominent and last at least a full day.

296.4x Bipolar Disorder, Manic

Diagnostic criterion.

Currently (or most recently) in a manic episode (p. 95). (If there has been a previous manic episode, the current episode need not meet the full criteria for a manic episode.)

296.5x Bipolar Disorder, Depressed

Diagnostic criteria.

A. Has had one or more manic episodes (p. 95).

B. Currently (or most recently) in a major depressive episode (p. 97). (If there has been a previous major depressive episode, the current episode of depression need not meet the full criteria for a major depressive episode.)

MAJOR DEPRESSION

296.2x Major Depression, Single Episode

296.3x Major Depression, Recurrent

Diagnostic criteria.

A. One or more major depressive episodes (p. 97).

B. Has never had a manic episode (p. 95) or hypomanic episode (see p. 104).

OTHER SPECIFIC AFFECTIVE DISORDERS

301.13 Cyclothymic Disorder

Differential diagnosis. Bipolar Disorder, major depressive episode, manic episode.

Diagnostic criteria.

A. During the past two years, numerous periods during which some symptoms characteristic of both the depressive and the manic syndromes were present but were not of sufficient severity and duration to meet the criteria for a major depressive or manic episode.

B. The depressive periods and hypomanic periods may be separated by periods of normal mood lasting as long as months at a time, they may be intermixed, or they may alternate.

C. During *depressive* periods there is depressed mood or loss of interest or pleasure in all, or almost all,	During *hypomanic* periods there is an elevated, expansive, or irritable mood and at least three of the following:

usual activities and pastimes, and at least three of the following:

(1)	insomnia or hypersomnia	decreased need for sleep
(2)	low energy or chronic fatigue	more energy than usual
(3)	feelings of inadequacy	inflated self-esteem
(4)	decreased effectiveness or productivity at school, work, or home	increased productivity, often associated with unusual and self-imposed working hours
(5)	decreased attention, concentration, or ability to think clearly	sharpened and unusually creative thinking
(6)	social withdrawal	uninhibited people-seeking (extreme gregariousness)
(7)	loss of interest in or enjoyment of sex	hypersexuality without recognition of possibility of painful consequences
(8)	restriction of involvement in pleasurable activities; guilt over past activities	excessive involvement in pleasurable activities with lack of concern for the high potential for painful consequences, e.g., buying sprees, foolish business investments, reckless driving
(9)	feeling slowed down	physical restlessness
(10)	less talkative than usual	more talkative than usual
(11)	pessimistic attitude toward the future, or brooding about past events	overoptimism or exaggeration of past achievements

(12) tearfulness or crying	inappropriate laughing, joking, punning

D. Absence of psychotic features such as delusions, hallucinations, incoherence, or loosening of associations.

E. Not due to any other mental disorder, such as partial remission of Bipolar Disorder. However, Cyclothymic Disorder may precede Bipolar Disorder.

300.40 Dysthymic Disorder (or Depressive Neurosis)

Differential diagnosis. Major Depression; normal fluctuations of mood; chronic mental disorders, such as Obsessive Compulsive Disorder or Alcohol Dependence, when associated with depressive symptoms.

Diagnostic criteria.

A. During the past two years (or one year for children and adolescents) the individual has been bothered most or all of the time by symptoms characteristic of the depressive syndrome that are not of sufficient severity and duration to meet the criteria for a major depressive episode.

B. The manifestations of the depressive syndrome may be relatively persistent or separated by periods of normal mood lasting a few days to a few weeks, but no more than a few months at a time.

C. During the depressive periods there is either prominent depressed mood (e.g., sad, blue, down in the dumps, low) or marked loss of interest or pleasure in all, or almost all, usual activities and pastimes.

D. During the depressive periods at least three of the following symptoms are present:

(1) insomnia or hypersomnia
(2) low energy level or chronic tiredness
(3) feelings of inadequacy, loss of self-esteem, or self-deprecation
(4) decreased effectiveness or productivity at

school, work, or home

(5) decreased attention, concentration, or ability to think clearly

(6) social withdrawal

(7) loss of interest in or enjoyment of pleasurable activities

(8) irritability or excessive anger (in children, expressed toward parents or caretakers)

(9) inability to respond with apparent pleasure to praise or rewards

(10) less active or talkative than usual, or feels slowed down or restless

(11) pessimistic attitude toward the future, brooding about past events, or feeling sorry for self

(12) tearfulness or crying

(13) recurrent thoughts of death or suicide

E. There are no psychotic features, such as delusions, hallucinations, or incoherence.

F. If the disturbance is superimposed on another mental disorder or a preexisting mental disorder, such as Obsessive Compulsive Disorder or Alcohol Dependence, the depressed mood, by virtue of its intensity or effect on functioning, can be clearly distinguished from the individual's usual mood.

ATYPICAL AFFECTIVE DISORDERS

296.70 Atypical Bipolar Disorder

This is a residual category for individuals with manic features that cannot be classified as Bipolar Disorder or as Cyclothymic Disorder. For example, an individual who previously had a major depressive episode, now has an episode of illness with some manic features (hypomanic episode), but not of sufficient severity and duration to meet the criteria for a manic episode. Such cases have been referred to as "Bipolar II."

296.82 Atypical Depression

This is a residual category for individuals with depressive symptoms who cannot be diagnosed as having Major or Other Specific Affective Disorder or Adjustment Disorder. Examples include the following:

(1) A distinct and sustained episode of the full depressive syndrome in an individual with Schizophrenia, Residual Type, that develops without an activation of the psychotic symptoms.
(2) A disorder that fulfills the criteria for Dysthymic Disorder; however, there have been intermittent periods of normal mood lasting more than a few months.
(3) A brief episode of depression that does not meet the criteria for a Major Affective Disorder and that is apparently not reactive to psychosocial stress, so that it cannot be classified as an Adjustment Disorder.

Anxiety Disorders

PHOBIC DISORDERS (OR PHOBIC NEUROSES)

300.2x Agoraphobia

Differential diagnosis. Phobic avoidance of certain situations in Schizophrenia, Major Depression, Obsessive Compulsive Disorder, Paranoid Personality Disorder.

Diagnostic criteria.

A. The individual has marked fear of and thus avoids being alone or in public places from which escape might be difficult or help not available in case of sudden incapacitation, e.g., crowds, tunnels, bridges, public transportation.

B. There is increasing constriction of normal activities until the fears or avoidance behavior dominate the individual's life.

C. Not due to a major depressive episode, Obsessive Compulsive Disorder, Paranoid Personality Disorder, or Schizophrenia.

300.21 Agoraphobia with Panic Attacks

A history of panic attacks whether or not currently present.

300.22 Agoraphobia without Panic Attacks

No history of panic attacks.

300.23 Social Phobia

Differential diagnosis. Avoidance of certain social situations that are normally a source of some distress, e.g. normal fear of public speaking, Schizophrenia, Major Depression, Obsessive Compulsive Disorder, Paranoid and Avoidant Personality Disorders, Simple Phobia.

Diagnostic criteria.

A. A persistent irrational fear of, and compelling

desire to avoid, a situation in which the individual is exposed to possible scrutiny by others and fears that he or she may act in a way that will be humiliating or embarrassing.

B. Significant distress because of the disturbance, and recognition by the individual that his or her fear is excessive or unreasonable.

C. Not due to another mental disorder, such as Major Depression or Avoidant Personality Disorder.

300.29 Simple Phobia

Differential diagnosis. Schizophrenia, Obsessive Compulsive Disorder.

Diagnostic criteria.

A. A persistent, irrational fear of, and compelling desire to avoid, an object or a situation other than being alone, or in public places away from home (Agoraphobia), or of humiliation or embarrassment in certain social situations (Social Phobia). Phobic objects are often animals, and phobic situations frequently involve heights or closed spaces.

B. Significant distress from the disturbance and recognition by the individual that his or her fear is excessive or unreasonable.

C. Not due to another mental disorder, such as Schizophrenia or Obsessive Compulsive Disorder.

ANXIETY STATES (OR ANXIETY NEUROSES)

300.01 Panic Disorder

Differential diagnosis. Physical disorders, such as hypoglycemia, pheochromocytoma, and hyperthyroidism; withdrawal from some substances, such as from barbiturates; substance intoxications, such as due to caffeine or amphetamine; Schizophrenia; Major Depression; Somatization Disorder; Generalized Anxiety Disorder; Simple or Social Phobia.

Diagnostic criteria.

A. At least three panic attacks within a three-week period in circumstances other than during marked physical exertion or in a life-threatening situation. The attacks are not precipitated only by exposure to a circumscribed phobic stimulus.

B. Panic attacks are manifested by discrete periods of apprehension or fear, and at least four of the following symptoms appear during each attack:

(1) dyspnea
(2) palpitations
(3) chest pain or discomfort
(4) choking or smothering sensations
(5) dizziness, vertigo, or unsteady feelings
(6) feelings of unreality
(7) paresthesias (tingling in hands or feet)
(8) hot and cold flashes
(9) sweating
(10) faintness
(11) trembling or shaking
(12) fear of dying, going crazy, or doing something uncontrolled during an attack

C. Not due to a physical disorder or another mental disorder, such as Major Depression, Somatization Disorder, or Schizophrenia.

D. The disorder is not associated with Agoraphobia (p. 107).

300.02 Generalized Anxiety Disorder

Differential diagnosis. Physical disorders, such as hyperthyroidism; Organic Mental Disorders, such as Caffeine Intoxication; Adjustment Disorder with Anxious Mood; Schizophrenia; Depressive Disorders; Hypochondriasis; Obsessive Compulsive Disorder; Panic Disorder.

Diagnostic criteria.

A. Generalized, persistent anxiety is manifested by symptoms from three of the following four categories:

(1) *motor tension:* shakiness, jitteriness, jumpiness, trembling, tension, muscle aches, fatigability, inability to relax, eyelid twitch, furrowed brow, strained face, fidgeting, restlessness, easy startle
(2) *autonomic hyperactivity:* sweating, heart pounding or racing, cold clammy hands, dry mouth, dizziness, light-headedness, paresthesias (tingling in hands or feet), upset stomach, hot or cold spells, frequent urination, diarrhea, discomfort in the pit of the stomach, lump in the throat, flushing, pallor, high resting pulse and respiration rate
(3) *apprehensive expectation:* anxiety, worry, fear, rumination, and anticipation of misfortune to self or others
(4) *vigilance and scanning:* hyperattentiveness resulting in distractibility, difficulty in concentrating, insomnia, feeling "on edge," irritability, impatience

B. The anxious mood has been continuous for at least one month.

C. Not due to another mental disorder, such as a Depressive Disorder or Schizophrenia.

D. At least 18 years of age.

300.30 Obsessive Compulsive Disorder (or Obsessive Compulsive Neurosis)

Differential diagnosis. Obsessive brooding, rumination, or preoccupation; Schizophrenia; Major Depression; Tourette's Disorder; Organic Mental Disorder.

Diagnostic criteria.

A. Either obsessions or compulsions:

Obsessions: recurrent, persistent ideas, thoughts, images, or impulses that are ego-dystonic, i.e., they are not experienced as voluntarily produced, but rather as thoughts that invade consciousness and are experienced as senseless or repugnant.

Attempts are made to ignore or suppress them.

Compulsions: repetitive and seemingly purposeful behaviors that are performed according to certain rules or in a stereotyped fashion. The behavior is not an end in itself, but is designed to produce or prevent some future event or situation. However, either the activity is not connected in a realistic way with what it is designed to produce or prevent, or may be clearly excessive. The act is performed with a sense of subjective compulsion coupled with a desire to resist the compulsion (at least initially). The individual generally recognizes the senselessness of the behavior (this may not be true for young children) and does not derive pleasure from carrying out the activity, although it provides a release of tension.

B. The obsessions or compulsions are a significant source of distress to the individual or interfere with social or role functioning.

C. Not due to another mental disorder, such as Tourette's Disorder, Schizophrenia, Major Depression, or Organic Mental Disorder.

Post-traumatic Stress Disorder

Differential diagnosis. Adjustment Disorder with Anxious Mood.

Diagnostic criteria.

A. Existence of a recognizable stressor that would evoke significant symptoms of distress in almost anyone.

B. Reexperiencing of the trauma as evidenced by at least one of the following:

(1) recurrent and intrusive recollections of the event
(2) recurrent dreams of the event
(3) sudden acting or feeling as if the traumatic event were reoccurring, because of an association with an environmental or ideational stimulus

C. Numbing of responsiveness to or reduced involvement with the external world, beginning some time after the trauma, as shown by at least one of the following:

(1) markedly diminished interest in one or more significant activities
(2) feeling of detachment or estrangement from others
(3) constricted affect

D. At least two of the following symptoms that were not present before the trauma:

(1) hyperalertness or exaggerated startle response
(2) sleep disturbance
(3) guilt about surviving when others have not, or about behavior required for survival
(4) memory impairment or trouble concentrating
(5) avoidance of activities that arouse recollection of the traumatic event
(6) intensification of symptoms by exposure to events that symbolize or resemble the traumatic event

Subtypes

308.30 Post-traumatic Stress Disorder, Acute

A. Onset of symptoms within six months of the trauma.

B. Duration of symptoms of less than six months.

309.81 Post-traumatic Stress Disorder, Chronic or Delayed

Either of the following, or both:

(1) duration of symptoms of six months or more (chronic)
(2) onset of symptoms at least six months after the trauma (delayed)

300.00 Atypical Anxiety Disorder

This category should be used when the individual appears to have an Anxiety Disorder that does not meet the criteria for any of the above specified conditions.

300.81 Somatization Disorder

Differential diagnosis. Physical disorders that present with vague, multiple, and confusing somatic symptoms, e.g., hyperparathyroidism, porphyria, multiple sclerosis, and systemic lupus erythematosus; Schizophrenia with multiple somatic delusions; Dysthymic Disorder; Generalized Anxiety Disorder; Major Depression; Panic Disorder; Conversion Disorder; Factitious Disorder with Physical Symptoms.

Diagnostic criteria.

A. A history of physical symptoms of several years' duration, beginning before the age of 30.

B. Complaints of at least 14 symptoms for women and 12 for men from the 37 symptoms listed below. To count a symptom as present the individual must report that the symptom caused him or her to take medicine (other than aspirin), alter his or her life pattern, or see a physician. The symptoms, in the judgment of the clinician, are not adequately explained by physical disorder or physical injury and are not side effects of medication, drugs or alcohol. The clinician need not be convinced that the symptom was actually present, e.g., that the individual actually vomited throughout her entire pregnancy; report of the symptom by the individual is sufficient.

Sickly: Believes that he or she has been sickly for a good part of his or her life.

Conversion or pseudoneurological symptoms: Difficulty swallowing, loss of voice, deafness, double vision, blurred vision, blindness, fainting or loss of consciousness, memory loss, seizures or convulsions, trouble walking, paralysis or muscle weakness, urinary retention or difficulty urinating.

Gastrointestinal symptoms: Abdominal pain, nausea, vomiting spells (other than during pregnancy), bloating (gassy), intolerance (e.g., gets sick) of a variety of foods, diarrhea.

Female reproductive symptoms: Judged by the individual as occurring more frequently or severely than in most women: painful menstruation, menstrual irregularity, excessive bleeding, severe vomiting throughout pregnancy or causing hospitalization during pregnancy.

Psychosexual symptoms: For the major part of the individual's life after opportunities for sexual activity: sexual indifference, lack of pleasure during intercourse, pain during intercourse.

Pain: Pain in back, joints, extremities, genital area (other than during intercourse); pain on urination; other pain (other than headaches).

Cardiopulmonary symptoms: Shortness of breath, palpitations, chest pain, dizziness.

300.11 Conversion Disorder (or Hysterical Neurosis, Conversion Type)

Differential diagnosis. Physical disorders that present with vague, multiple somatic symptoms, such as multiple sclerosis, systemic lupus erythematosus; undiagnosed physical disorder; physical disorders in which psychological factors often play an important role, such as irritable colon or bronchial asthma; Somatization Disorder; Schizophrenia; Psychogenic Pain Disorder; Hypochondriasis, Factitious Disorder with Physical Symptoms; Malingering.

Diagnostic criteria.

A. The predominant disturbance is a loss of or alteration in physical functioning suggesting a physical disorder.

B. Psychological factors are judged to be etiologically involved in the symptom, as evidenced by one of the following:

(1) there is a temporal relationship between an environmental stimulus that is apparently related to a psychological conflict or need and the initiation or exacerbation of the symptom

(2) the symptom enables the individual to avoid some activity that is noxious to him or her

(3) the symptom enables the individual to get support from the environment that otherwise might not be forthcoming

C. It has been determined that the symptom is *not* under voluntary control.

D. The symptom cannot, after appropriate investigation, be explained by a known physical disorder or pathophysiological mechanism.

E. The symptom is not limited to pain or to a disturbance in sexual functioning.

F. Not due to Somatization Disorder or Schizophrenia.

307.80 Psychogenic Pain Disorder

Differential diagnosis. Dramatic presentation of organic pain, pain associated with muscle contraction headaches ("tension headaches"), Somatization Disorder, Depressive Disorders, Schizophrenia, Malingering.

Diagnostic criteria.

A. Severe and prolonged pain is the predominant disturbance.

B. The pain presented as a symptom is inconsistent with the anatomic distribution of the nervous system; after extensive evaluation, no organic pathology or pathophysiological mechanism can be found to account for the pain; or, when there is some related organic pathology, the complaint of pain is grossly in excess of what would be expected from the physical findings.

C. Psychological factors are judged to be etiologically involved in the pain, as evidenced by at least one of the following:

(1) a temporal relationship between an environmental stimulus that is apparently related to a psychological conflict or need and the initiation or exacerbation of the pain
(2) the pain's enabling the individual to avoid some activity that is noxious to him or her

(3) the pain's enabling the individual to get support from the environment that otherwise might not be forthcoming

D. Not due to another mental disorder.

300.70 Hypochondriasis (or Hypochondriacal Neurosis)

Differential diagnosis. True organic disease; some psychotic disorders, such as Schizophrenia and Major Depression with Psychotic Features; Dysthymic Disorder, Panic Disorder, Generalized Anxiety Disorder, Obsessive Compulsive Disorder, Somatization Disorder.

Diagnostic criteria.

A. The predominant disturbance is an unrealistic interpretation of physical signs or sensations as abnormal, leading to preoccupation with the fear or belief of having a serious disease.

B. Thorough physical evaluation does not support the diagnosis of any physical disorder that can account for the physical signs or sensations or for the individual's unrealistic interpretation of them.

C. The unrealistic fear or belief of having a disease persists despite medical reassurance and causes impairment in social or occupational functioning.

D. Not due to any other mental disorder such as Schizophrenia, Affective Disorder, or Somatization Disorder.

300.70 Atypical Somatoform Disorder

This is a residual category to be used when the predominant disturbance is the presentation of physical symptoms or complaints not explainable on the basis of demonstrable organic findings or a known pathophysiological mechanism and apparently linked to psychological factors.

An example of cases that can be classified here include those of individuals who are preoccupied with some imagined defect in physical appearance that is out of proportion to any actual physical abnormality that may exist. This syndrome has sometimes been termed "Dysmorphophobia."

Dissociative Disorders (or Hysterical Neuroses, Dissociative Type)

300.12 Psychogenic Amnesia

Differential diagnosis. Postconcussion amnesia, epilepsy, Organic Mental Disorders such as Dementia or Substance-induced Intoxication, Alcohol Amnestic Disorder, Malingering.

Diagnostic criteria.

A. Sudden inability to recall important personal information that is too extensive to be explained by ordinary forgetfulness.

B. The disturbance is not due to an Organic Mental Disorder (e.g., blackouts during Alcohol Intoxication).

300.13 Psychogenic Fugue

Differential diagnosis. Temporal lobe epilepsy, Organic Mental Disorders, Psychogenic Amnesia, Malingering.

Diagnostic criteria.

A. Sudden unexpected travel away from home or one's customary place of work, with inability to recall one's past.

B. Assumption of a new identity (partial or complete).

C. The disturbance is not due to an Organic Mental Disorder.

300.14 Multiple Personality

Differential diagnosis. Psychogenic Fugue, Psychogenic Amnesia, psychotic disorders such as Schizophrenia, Malingering.

Diagnostic criteria.

A. The existence within the individual of two or more distinct personalities, each of which is dominant at a particular time.

B. The personality that is dominant at any particular time determines the individual's behavior.

C. Each individual personality is complex and integrated with its own unique behavior patterns and social relationships.

300.60 Depersonalization Disorder (or Depersonalization Neurosis)

Differential diagnosis. Epilepsy, depersonalization without social or occupational impairment, Schizophrenia, Affective Disorders, Organic Mental Disorders, Anxiety Disorders, Personality Disorders.

Diagnostic criteria.

A. One or more episodes of depersonalization sufficient to produce significant impairment in social or occupational functioning.

B. The symptom is not due to any other disorder, such as Schizophrenia, Affective Disorder, Organic Mental Disorder, Anxiety Disorder, or epilepsy.

300.15 Atypical Dissociative Disorder

This is a residual category to be used for individuals who appear to have a Dissociative Disorder but do not satisfy the criteria for a specific Dissociative Disorder. Examples include trancelike states, derealization unaccompanied by depersonalization, and those more prolonged dissociated states that may occur in persons who have been subjected to periods of prolonged and intense coercive persuasion (brainwashing, thought reform, and indoctrination while the captive of terrorists or cultists).

GENDER IDENTITY DISORDERS

302.5x Transsexualism

Differential diagnosis. Effeminate homosexuality, physical intersex, Schizophrenia, Transvestism.

Diagnostic criteria.

A. Sense of discomfort and inappropriateness about one's anatomic sex.

B. Wish to be rid of one's own genitals and to live as a member of the other sex.

C. The disturbance has been continuous (not limited to periods of stress) for at least two years.

D. Absence of physical intersex or genetic abnormality.

E. Not due to another mental disorder, such as Schizophrenia.

Fifth-digit code numbers and subclassification:

The predominant prior sexual history is recorded in the fifth digit as:

1=asexual
2=homosexual (same anatomic sex)
3=heterosexual (other anatomic sex)
0=unspecified

302.60 Gender Identity Disorder of Childhood

Differential diagnosis. Children whose behavior merely does not fit the cultural stereotype of masculinity or femininity.

Diagnostic criteria.

For Females:

A. Strongly and persistently stated desire to be a

boy, or insistence that she is a boy (not merely a desire for any perceived cultural advantages from being a boy).

B. Persistent repudiation of female anatomic structures, as manifested by at least one of the following repeated assertions:

(1) that she will grow up to become a man (not merely in role)
(2) that she is biologically unable to become pregnant
(3) that she will not develop breasts
(4) that she has no vagina
(5) that she has, or will grow, a penis

C. Onset of the disturbance before puberty. (For adults and adolescents, see Atypical Gender Identity Disorder.)

For Males:

A. Strongly and persistently stated desire to be a girl, or insistence that he is a girl.

B. Either (1) or (2):

(1) Persistent repudiation of male anatomic structures, as manifested by at least one of the following repeated assertions:

(*a*) that he will grow up to become a woman (not merely in role)
(*b*) that his penis or testes are disgusting or will disappear
(*c*) that it would be better not to have a penis or testes

(2) Preoccupation with female stereotypical activities as manifested by a preference for either cross-dressing or simulating female attire, or by a compelling desire to participate in the games and pastimes of girls.

C. Onset of the disturbance before puberty. (For adults and adolescents, see Atypical Gender Identity Disorder.)

302.85 Atypical Gender Identity Disorder

This is a residual category for coding disorders in gender identity that are not classifiable as a specific Gender Identity Disorder.

PARAPHILIAS

302.81 Fetishism

Differential diagnosis. Nonpathological sexual experimentation with nonhuman objects, Transvestism.

Diagnostic criteria.

A. The use of nonliving objects (fetishes) is a repeatedly preferred or exclusive method of achieving sexual excitement.

B. The fetishes are not limited to articles of female clothing used in cross-dressing (Transvestism) or to objects designed to be used for the purpose of sexual stimulation (e.g., vibrator).

302.30 Transvestism

Differential diagnosis. Transsexualism, cross-dressing for the relief of tension or gender discomfort, cross-dressing in male homosexuality, female impersonators.

Diagnostic criteria.

A. Recurrent and persistent cross-dressing by a heterosexual male.

B. Use of cross-dressing for the purpose of sexual excitement, at least initially, in the course of the disorder.

C. Intense frustration when the cross-dressing is interfered with.

D. Does not meet the criteria for Transsexualism.

302.10 Zoophilia

Differential diagnosis. Nonpathological sexual experimentation with animals.

Diagnostic criteria.

The act or fantasy of engaging in sexual activity with animals is a repeatedly preferred or exclusive method of achieving sexual excitement.

302.20 Pedophilia

Differential diagnosis. Isolated sexual acts with children associated with stress or Mental Retardation, Organic Personality Syndrome, Alcohol Intoxication, Schizophrenia.

Diagnostic criteria.

A. The act or fantasy of engaging in sexual activity with prepubertal children is a repeatedly preferred or exclusive method of achieving sexual excitement.

B. If the individual is an adult, the prepubertal children are at least ten years younger than the individual. If the individual is a late adolescent, no precise age difference is required, and clinical judgment must take into account the age difference as well as the sexual maturity of the child.

302.40 Exhibitionism

Differential diagnosis. Repeated exposure without experiencing sexual excitement.

Diagnostic criteria.

Repetitive acts of exposing the genitals to an unsuspecting stranger for the purpose of achieving sexual excitement, with no attempt at further sexual activity with the stranger.

302.82 Voyeurism

Differential diagnosis. Watching pornography.

Diagnostic criteria.

A. The individual repeatedly observes unsuspecting

people who are either naked, in the act of disrobing, or engaging in sexual activity and no sexual activity with the observed people is sought.

B. The observing is the repeatedly preferred or exclusive method of achieving sexual excitement.

302.83 Sexual Masochism

Differential diagnosis. Masochistic fantasies, masochistic personality traits.

Diagnostic criteria.

Either (1) or (2):

(1) a preferred or exclusive mode of producing sexual excitement is to be humiliated, bound, beaten, or otherwise made to suffer

(2) the individual has intentionally participated in an activity in which he or she was physically harmed or his or her life was threatened, in order to produce sexual excitement

302.84 Sexual Sadism

Differential diagnosis. Rape or other sexual assault not due to Sexual Sadism.

Diagnostic criteria.

One of the following:

(1) on a nonconsenting partner, the individual has repeatedly intentionally inflicted psychological or physical suffering in order to produce sexual excitement

(2) with a consenting partner, the preferred or exclusive mode of achieving sexual excitement combines humiliation with simulated or mildly injurious bodily suffering

(3) on a consenting partner, bodily injury that is extensive, permanent, or possibly mortal is inflicted in order to achieve sexual excitement

302.90 Atypical Paraphilia

This is a residual category for individuals with

Paraphilias that cannot be classified in any of the other categories. Such conditions include: Coprophilia (feces); Frotteurism (rubbing); Klismaphilia (enema); Mysophilia (filth); Necrophilia (corpse); Telephone Scatologia (lewdness); and Urophilia (urine).

PSYCHOSEXUAL DYSFUNCTIONS

302.71 Inhibited Sexual Desire

Differential diagnosis. Physical disorder or another Axis I mental disorder that completely accounts for the disturbance, inadequate sexual stimulation.

Diagnostic criteria.

A. Persistent and pervasive inhibition of sexual desire. The judgment of inhibition is made by the clinician's taking into account factors that affect sexual desire such as age, sex, health, intensity and frequency of sexual desire, and the context of the individual's life. In actual practice this diagnosis will rarely be made unless the lack of desire is a source of distress to either the individual or his or her partner. Frequently this category will be used in conjunction with one or more of the other Psychosexual Dysfunction categories.

B. The disturbance is not caused exclusively by organic factors (e.g., physical disorder or medication) and is not due to another Axis I disorder.

302.72 Inhibited Sexual Excitement

Diagnostic criteria.

A. Recurrent and persistent inhibition of sexual excitement during sexual activity, manifested by:

In males, partial or complete failure to attain or maintain erection until completion of the sexual act, or

In females, partial or complete failure to attain or maintain the lubrication-swelling response of sexual excitement until completion of the sexual act.

B. A clinical judgment that the individual engages in sexual activity that is adequate in focus, intensity, and duration.

C. The disturbance is not caused exclusively by organic factors (e.g., physical disorder or medication) and is not due to another Axis I disorder.

302.73 Inhibited Female Orgasm

Diagnostic criteria.

A. Recurrent and persistent inhibition of the female orgasm as manifested by a delay in or absence of orgasm following a normal sexual excitement phase during sexual activity that is judged by the clinician to be adequate in focus, intensity, and duration. The same individual may also meet the criteria for Inhibited Sexual Excitement if at other times there is a problem with the excitement phase of sexual activity. In such cases both categories of Psychosexual Dysfunction should be noted.

Some women are able to experience orgasm during noncoital clitoral stimulation, but are unable to experience it during coitus in the absence of manual clitoral stimulation. There is evidence to suggest that in some instances this represents a pathological inhibition that justifies this diagnosis whereas in other instances it represents a normal variation of the female sexual response. This difficult judgment is assisted by a thorough sexual evaluation, which may even require a trial of treatment.

B. The disturbance is not caused exclusively by organic factors (e.g., physical disorder or medication) and is not due to another Axis I disorder.

302.74 Inhibited Male Orgasm

Diagnostic criteria.

A. Recurrent and persistent inhibition of the male orgasm as manifested by a delay in or absence of ejaculation following an adequate phase of sexual excitement. The same individual may also meet the criteria for Inhibited Sexual Excitement if at other times there is a problem with the excitement phase of sexual activity. In such cases both categories of Psychosexual Dysfunction should be noted.

B. The disturbance is not caused exclusively by organic factors (e.g, physical disorder or medication) and is not due to another Axis I disorder.

302.75 Premature Ejaculation

Diagnostic criteria.

A. Ejaculation occurs before the individual wishes it, because of recurrent and persistent absence of reasonable voluntary control of ejaculation and orgasm during sexual activity. The judgment of "reasonable control" is made by the clinician's taking into account factors that affect duration of the excitement phase, such as age, novelty of the sexual partner, and the frequency and duration of coitus.

B. The disturbance is not due to another Axis I disorder.

302.76 Functional Dyspareunia

Diagnostic criteria.

A. Coitus is associated with recurrent and persistent genital pain, in either the male or the female.

B. The disturbance is not caused exclusively by a physical disorder, and is not due to lack of lubrication, Functional Vaginismus, or another Axis I disorder.

306.51 Functional Vaginismus

Diagnostic criteria.

A. There is a history of recurrent and persistent involuntary spasm of the musculature of the outer third of the vagina that interferes with coitus.

B. The disturbance is not caused exclusively by a physical disorder, and is not due to another Axis I disorder.

302.70 Atypical Psychosexual Dysfunction

This category is for Psychosexual Dysfunctions that cannot be classified as a specific Psychosexual Dysfunction. An example would be no erotic sensations or even complete anesthesia despite normal physiological components of sexual excitement and orgasm. Another example would be a female analogue of Premature Ejaculation.

OTHER PSYCHOSEXUAL DISORDERS

302.00 Ego-dystonic Homosexuality

Differential diagnosis. Homosexuality that is ego-syntonic, Inhibited Sexual Desire.

Diagnostic criteria.

A. The individual complains that heterosexual arousal is persistently absent or weak and significantly interferes with initiating or maintaining wanted heterosexual relationships.

B. There is a sustained pattern of homosexual arousal that the individual explicitly states has been unwanted and a persistent source of distress.

302.89 Psychosexual Disorder Not Elsewhere Classified

This is a residual category for disorders whose chief manifestations are psychological disturbances related to sexuality not covered by any of the other specific categories in the diagnostic class of Psychosexual Disorders. In rare instances this category may be used concurrently with one of the specific diagnoses when both diagnoses are necessary to explain or describe the clinical disturbance.

Examples include the following:

(1) marked feelings of inadequacy related to self-imposed standards of masculinity or femininity, such as body habitus, size and shape of sex organs, or sexual performance;

(2) impaired pleasure during the normal physiological pelvic response of orgasm;
(3) distress about a pattern of repeated sexual conquests with a succession of individuals who exist only as things to be used (Don Juanism and nymphomania);
(4) confusion about preferred sexual orientation.

300.16 Factitious Disorder with Psychological Symptoms

Differential diagnosis. Dementia, true psychosis such as Brief Reactive Psychosis or Schizophreniform Disorder, Malingering.

Diagnostic criteria.

A. The production of psychological symptoms is apparently under the individual's voluntary control.

B. The symptoms produced are not explained by any other mental disorder (although they may be superimposed on one).

C. The individual's goal is apparently to assume the "patient" role and is not otherwise understandable in light of the individual's environmental circumstances (as is the case in Malingering).

Factitious Disorder With Physical Symptoms

301.51 Chronic Factitious Disorder with Physical Symptoms

Differential diagnosis. True physical disorder, Somatoform Disorders, Malingering, Antisocial Personality Disorder, Schizophrenia.

Diagnostic criteria.

A. Plausible presentation of physical symptoms that are apparently under the individual's voluntary control to such a degree that there are multiple hospitalizations.

B. The individual's goal is apparently to assume the "patient" role and is not otherwise understandable in light of the individual's environmental circumstances (as is the case in Malingering).

300.19 Atypical Factitious Disorder with Physical Symptoms

This is a residual category for Factitious Disorders with Physical Symptoms that do not fulfill the criteria for Chronic Factitious Disorder with Physical Symptoms.

Usually individuals with Atypical Factitious Disorders with Physical Symptoms do not require hospitalization. Examples include dermatitis artifacta (induced by excoriation or chemicals) and voluntary dislocation of the shoulder.

Disorders of Impulse Control Not Elsewhere Classified

312.31 Pathological Gambling

Differential diagnosis. Social gambling, manic or hypomanic episode, Antisocial Personality Disorder.

Diagnostic criteria.

A. The individual is chronically and progressively unable to resist impulses to gamble.

B. Gambling compromises, disrupts, or damages family, personal, and vocational pursuits, as indicated by at least three of the following:

(1) arrest for forgery, fraud, embezzlement, or income tax evasion due to attempts to obtain money for gambling

(2) default on debts or other financial responsibilities

(3) disrupted family or spouse relationship due to gambling

(4) borrowing of money from illegal sources (loan sharks)

(5) inability to account for loss of money or to produce evidence of winning money, if this is claimed

(6) loss of work due to absenteeism in order to pursue gambling activity

(7) necessity for another person to provide money to relieve a desperate financial situation

C. The gambling is not due to Antisocial Personality Disorder.

312.32 Kleptomania

Differential diagnosis. Ordinary stealing, Malingering, Conduct Disorder, Antisocial Personality Disorder, manic episodes, Schizophrenia, Organic Mental Disorders.

Diagnostic criteria.

A. Recurrent failure to resist impulses to steal objects that are not for immediate use or their monetary value.

B. Increasing sense of tension before committing the act.

C. An experience of either pleasure or release at the time of committing the theft.

D. Stealing is done without long-term planning and assistance from, or collaboration with, others.

E. Not due to Conduct Disorder or Antisocial Personality Disorder.

312.33 Pyromania

Differential diagnosis. Young children's experimentation and fascination with matches, Conduct Disorder, Antisocial Personality Disorder, incendiary acts of sabotage, Schizophrenia, Organic Mental Disorders.

Diagnostic criteria.

A. Recurrent failure to resist impulses to set fires.

B. Increasing sense of tension before setting the fire.

C. An experience of either intense pleasure, gratification, or release at the time of committing the act.

D. Lack of motivation, such as monetary gain or sociopolitical ideology, for setting fires.

E. Not due to an Organic Mental Disorder, Schizophrenia, Antisocial Personality Disorder, or Conduct Disorder.

312.34 Intermittent Explosive Disorder

Differential diagnosis. Antisocial Personality Disorder, Dissociative Disorder, Paranoid Disorder, Schizophrenia.

Diagnostic criteria.

A. Several discrete episodes of loss of control of

aggressive impulses resulting in serious assault or destruction of property.

B. Behavior that is grossly out of proportion to any precipitating psychosocial stressor.

C. Absence of signs of generalized impulsivity or aggressiveness between episodes.

D. Not due to Schizophrenia, Antisocial Personality Disorder, or Conduct Disorder.

312.35 Isolated Explosive Disorder

Differential diagnosis. See Intermittent Explosive Disorder (above).

Diagnostic criteria.

A. A single, discrete episode in which failure to resist an impulse led to a single, violent externally directed act that had a catastrophic impact on others.

B. The degree of aggressivity expressed during the episode was grossly out of proportion to any precipitating psychosocial stressor.

C. Before the episode there were no signs of generalized impulsivity or aggressiveness.

D. Not due to Schizophrenia, Antisocial Personality Disorder, or Conduct Disorder.

312.39 Atypical Impulse Control Disorder

This category is for Disorders of Impulse Control that cannot be classified elsewhere.

Differential diagnosis. Conditions Not Attributable to a Mental Disorder, Personality Disorders exacerbated by stress, Psychological Factors Affecting Physical Condition.

Diagnostic criteria.

A. A maladaptive reaction to an identifiable psychosocial stressor, that occurs within three months of the onset of the stressor.

B. The maladaptive nature of the reaction is indicated by either of the following:

(1) impairment in social or occupational functioning
(2) symptoms that are in excess of a normal and expectable reaction to the stressor

C. The disturbance is not merely one instance of a pattern of overreaction to stress or an exacerbation of one of the mental disorders previously described.

D. It is assumed that the disturbance will eventually remit after the stressor ceases or, if the stressor persists, when a new level of adaptation is achieved.

E. The disturbance does not meet the criteria for any of the specific disorders listed previously or for Uncomplicated Bereavement.

Types of Adjustment Disorder. Code predominant symptoms.

309.00 Adjustment Disorder with Depressed Mood

This category should be used when the predominant manifestation involves such symptoms as depressed mood, tearfulness, and hopelessness. The major differential is with Major Depression and Uncomplicated Bereavement.

309.24 Adjustment Disorder with Anxious Mood

This category should be used when the predominant

manifestation involves such symptoms as nervousness, worry, and jitteriness. The major differential is with Anxiety Disorders.

309.28 Adjustment Disorder with Mixed Emotional Features

This category should be used when the predominant manifestation involves various combinations of depression and anxiety or other emotions. The major differential is with Depressive and Anxiety Disorders. An example would be an adolescent who, after moving away from home and parental supervision, reacts with ambivalence, depression, anger, and signs of increased dependency.

309.30 Adjustment Disorder with Disturbance of Conduct

This category should be used when the predominant manifestation involves conduct in which there is violation of the rights of others or of major age-appropriate societal norms and rules. Examples: truancy, vandalism, reckless driving, fighting, defaulting on legal responsibilities. The major differential is with Conduct Disorder and Antisocial Personality Disorder.

309.40 Adjustment Disorder with Mixed Disturbance of Emotions and Conduct

This category should be used when the predominant manifestations involve both emotional features (e.g., depression, anxiety) and a disturbance of conduct (see above).

309.23 Adjustment Disorder with Work (or Academic) Inhibition

This category should be used when the predominant manifestation is an inhibition in work or academic functioning occurring in an individual whose previous work or academic performance has been adequate. Frequently there may also be varying mixtures of anxiety and depression. Examples include inability to study and to write papers or reports. The major differential is with Depressive Disorders and Anxiety Disorders.

309.83 Adjustment Disorder with Withdrawal

This category should be used when the predominant manifestation involves social withdrawal without significant depressed or anxious mood. The major differential is with Depressive Disorders.

309.90 Adjustment Disorder with Atypical Features

This category should be used when the predominant manifestation involves symptoms that cannot be coded in any of the specific categories.

Psychological Factors Affecting Physical Condition

Specify physical disorder on Axis III.

316.00 Psychological Factors Affecting Physical Condition

Differential diagnosis. Conversion Disorder.

Diagnostic criteria.

A. Psychologically meaningful environmental stimuli are temporally related to the initiation or exacerbation of a physical condition (recorded on Axis III).

B. The physical condition has either demonstrable organic pathology (e.g., rheumatoid arthritis) or a known pathophysiological process (e.g., migraine headache, vomiting).

C. The condition is not due to a Somatoform Disorder.

Personality Disorders

(NOTE: These are coded on Axis II.)

301.00 Paranoid Personality Disorder

Differential diagnosis. Paranoid Disorders; Schizophrenia, Paranoid Type; Antisocial Personality Disorder.

Diagnostic criteria.

The following are characteristic of the individual's current and long-term functioning, are not limited to episodes of illness, and cause either significant impairment in social or occupational functioning or subjective distress.

A. Pervasive, unwarranted suspiciousness and mistrust of people as indicated by at least three of the following:

(1) expectation of trickery or harm
(2) hypervigilance, manifested by continual scanning of the environment for signs of threat, or taking unneeded precautions
(3) guardedness or secretiveness
(4) avoidance of accepting blame even when warranted
(5) questioning the loyalty of others
(6) intense, narrowly focused searching for confirmation of bias, with loss of appreciation of total context
(7) overconcern with hidden motives and special meanings
(8) pathological jealousy

B. Hypersensitivity as indicated by at least two of the following:

(1) tendency to be easily slighted and quick to take offense
(2) exaggeration of difficulties, e.g., "making mountains out of molehills"
(3) readiness to counterattack when any threat

is perceived
(4) inability to relax

C. Restricted affectivity as indicated by at least two of the following:

(1) appearance of being "cold" and unemotional
(2) pride taken in always being objective, rational, and unemotional
(3) lack of a true sense of humor
(4) absence of passive, soft, tender, and sentimental feelings

D. Not due to another mental disorder such as Schizophrenia or a Paranoid Disorder.

301.20 Schizoid Personality Disorder

Differential diagnosis. Schizotypal Personality Disorder, Avoidant Personality Disorder, Schizoid Disorder of Childhood or Adolescence.

Diagnostic criteria.

The following are characteristic of the individual's current and long-term functioning, are not limited to episodes of illness, and cause either significant impairment in social or occupational functioning or subjective distress.

A. Emotional coldness and aloofness, and absence of warm, tender feelings for others.

B. Indifference to praise or criticism or to the feelings of others.

C. Close friendships with no more than one or two persons, including family members.

D. No eccentricities of speech, behavior, or thought characteristic of Schizotypal Personality Disorder.

E. Not due to a psychotic disorder such as Schizophrenia or Paranoid Disorder.

F. If under 18, does not meet the criteria for Schizoid Disorder of Childhood or Adolescence.

301.22 Schizotypal Personality Disorder

Differential diagnosis. Schizophrenia, Residual Type;

Schizoid Personality Disorder; Avoidant Personality Disorder; Depersonalization Disorder; Borderline Personality Disorder.

Diagnostic criteria.

The following are characteristic of the individual's current and long-term functioning, are not limited to episodes of illness, and cause either significant impairment in social or occupational functioning or subjective distress.

A. At least four of the following:

(1) magical thinking, e.g., superstitiousness, clairvoyance, telepathy, "6th sense," "others can feel my feelings" (in children and adolescents, bizarre fantasies or preoccupations)
(2) ideas of reference
(3) social isolation, e.g., no close friends or confidants, social contacts limited to essential everyday tasks
(4) recurrent illusions, sensing the presence of a force or person not actually present (e.g., "I felt as if my dead mother were in the room with me"), depersonalization, or derealization not associated with panic attacks
(5) odd speech (without loosening of associations or incoherence), e.g., speech that is digressive, vague, overelaborate, circumstantial, metaphorical
(6) inadequate rapport in face-to-face interaction due to constricted or inappropriate affect, e.g., aloof, cold
(7) suspiciousness or paranoid ideation
(8) undue social anxiety or hypersensitivity to real or imagined criticism

B. Does not meet the criteria for Schizophrenia.

301.50 Histrionic Personality Disorder

Differential diagnosis. Somatization Disorder, Borderline Personality Disorder.

Diagnostic criteria.

The following are characteristic of the individual's

current and long-term functioning, are not limited to episodes of illness, and cause either significant impairment in social or occupational functioning or subjective distress.

A. Behavior that is overly dramatic, reactive, and intensely expressed, as indicated by at least three of the following:

(1) self-dramatization, e.g., exaggerated expression of emotions
(2) incessant drawing of attention to oneself
(3) craving for activity and excitement
(4) overreaction to minor events
(5) irrational, angry outbursts or tantrums

B. Characteristic disturbances in interpersonal relationships as indicated by at least two of the following:

(1) perceived by others as shallow and lacking genuineness, even if superficially warm and charming
(2) egocentric, self-indulgent, and inconsiderate of others
(3) vain and demanding
(4) dependent, helpless, constantly seeking reassurance
(5) prone to manipulative suicidal threats, gestures, or attempts

301.81 Narcissistic Personality Disorder

Differential diagnosis. Borderline Personality Disorder, Histrionic Personality Disorder.

Diagnostic criteria.

The following are characteristic of the individual's current and long-term functioning, are not limited to episodes of illness, and cause either significant impairment in social or occupational functioning or subjective distress:

A. Grandiose sense of self-importance or uniqueness, e.g., exaggeration of achievements and talents, focus on the special nature of one's problems.

B. Preoccupation with fantasies of unlimited success, power, brilliance, beauty, or ideal love.

C. Exhibitionism: the person requires constant attention and admiration.

D. Cool indifference or marked feelings of rage, inferiority, shame, humiliation, or emptiness in response to criticism, indifference of others, or defeat.

E. At least two of the following are characteristic of disturbances in interpersonal relationships:

(1) entitlement: expectation of special favors without assuming reciprocal responsibilities, e.g., surprise and anger that people will not do what is wanted
(2) interpersonal exploitativeness: taking advantage of others to indulge own desires or for self-aggrandizement; disregard for the personal integrity and rights of others
(3) relationships that characteristically alternate between the extremes of overidealization and devaluation
(4) lack of empathy: inability to recognize how others feel, e.g., unable to appreciate the distress of someone who is seriously ill

301.70 Antisocial Personality Disorder

Differential diagnosis. Conduct Disorder, Adult Antisocial Behavior (V code), Severe Mental Retardation, Schizophrenia, manic episodes.

Diagnostic criteria.

A. Current age at least 18.

B. Onset before age 15 as indicated by a history of three or more of the following before that age:

(1) truancy (positive if it amounted to at least five days per year for at least two years, not including the last year of school)
(2) expulsion or suspension from school for misbehavior

(3) delinquency (arrested or referred to juvenile court because of behavior)
(4) running away from home overnight at least twice while living in parental or parental surrogate home
(5) persistent lying
(6) repeated sexual intercourse in a casual relationship
(7) repeated drunkenness or substance abuse
(8) thefts
(9) vandalism
(10) school grades markedly below expectations in relation to estimated or known IQ (may have resulted in repeating a year)
(11) chronic violations of rules at home and/or at school (other than truancy)
(12) initiation of fights

C. At least four of the following manifestations of the disorder since age 18:

(1) inability to sustain consistent work behavior, as indicated by any of the following: (*a*) too frequent job changes (e.g., three or more jobs in five years not accounted for by nature of job or economic or seasonal fluctuation), (*b*) significant unemployment (e.g., six months or more in five years when expected to work), (*c*) serious absenteeism from work (e.g., average three days or more of lateness or absence per month) (*d*) walking off several jobs without other jobs in sight (Note: Similar behavior in an academic setting during the last few years of school may substitute for this criterion in individuals who by reason of their age or circumstances have not had an opportunity to demonstrate occupational adjustment.)
(2) lack of ability to function as a responsible parent as evidenced by one or more of the following: (*a*) child's malnutrition, (*b*) child's illness resulting from lack of minimal hygiene standards, (*c*) failure to obtain medical care for a seriously ill child, (*d*) child's dependence on neighbors or nonresident relatives for food or shelter, (*e*) failure to arrange for a caretaker for a child under six when parent is away from home, (*f*) repeated

squandering, on personal items, of money required for household necessities

(3) failure to accept social norms with respect to lawful behavior, as indicated by any of the following: repeated thefts, illegal occupation (pimping, prostitution, fencing, selling drugs), multiple arrests, a felony conviction

(4) inability to maintain enduring attachment to a sexual partner as indicated by two or more divorces and/or separations (whether legally married or not), desertion of spouse, promiscuity (ten or more sexual partners within one year)

(5) irritability and aggressiveness as indicated by repeated physical fights or assault (not required by one's job or to defend someone or oneself), including spouse or child beating

(6) failure to honor financial obligations, as indicated by repeated defaulting on debts, failure to provide child support, failure to support other dependents on a regular basis

(7) failure to plan ahead, or impulsivity, as indicated by traveling from place to place without a prearranged job or clear goal for the period of travel or clear idea about when the travel would terminate, or lack of a fixed address for a month or more

(8) disregard for the truth as indicated by repeated lying, use of aliases, "conning" others for personal profit

(9) recklessness, as indicated by driving while intoxicated or recurrent speeding

D. A pattern of continuous antisocial behavior in which the rights of others are violated, with no intervening period of at least five years without antisocial behavior between age 15 and the present time (except when the individual was bedridden or confined in a hospital or penal institution).

E. Antisocial behavior is not due to either Severe Mental Retardation, Schizophrenia, or manic episodes.

301.83 Borderline Personality Disorder

Differential diagnosis. Identity Disorder, Cyclothymic

Disorder.

Diagnostic criteria.

The following are characteristic of the individual's current and long-term functioning, are not limited to episodes of illness, and cause either significant impairment in social or occupational functioning or subjective distress.

A. At least five of the following are required:

(1) impulsivity or unpredictability in at least two areas that are potentially self-damaging, e.g., spending, sex, gambling, substance use, shop-lifting, overeating, physically self-damaging acts
(2) a pattern of unstable and intense interpersonal relationships, e.g., marked shifts of attitude, idealization, devaluation, manipulation (consistently using others for one's own ends)
(3) inappropriate, intense anger or lack of control of anger, e.g., frequent displays of temper, constant anger
(4) identity disturbance manifested by uncertainty about several issues relating to identity, such as self-image, gender identity, long-term goals or career choice, friendship patterns, values, and loyalties, e.g., "Who am I", "I feel like I am my sister when I am good"
(5) affective instability: marked shifts from normal mood to depression, irritability, or anxiety, usually lasting a few hours and only rarely more than a few days, with a return to normal mood
(6) intolerance of being alone, e.g., frantic efforts to avoid being alone, depressed when alone
(7) physically self-damaging acts, e.g., suicidal gestures, self-mutilation, recurrent accidents or physical fights
(8) chronic feelings of emptiness or boredom

B. If under 18, does not meet the criteria for Identity Disorder.

301.82 Avoidant Personality Disorder

Differential diagnosis. Schizoid Personality Disorder,

Social Phobias, Avoidant Disorder of Childhood or Adolescence.

Diagnostic criteria.

The following are characteristic of the individual's current and long-term functioning, are not limited to episodes of illness, and cause either significant impairment in social or occupational functioning or subjective distress.

A. Hypersensitivity to rejection, e.g., apprehensively alert to signs of social derogation, interprets innocuous events as ridicule.

B. Unwillingness to enter into relationships unless given unusually strong guarantees of uncritical acceptance.

C. Social withdrawal, e.g., distances self from close personal attachments, engages in peripheral social and vocational roles.

D. Desire for affection and acceptance.

E. Low self-esteem, e.g., devalues self-achievements and is overly dismayed by personal shortcomings.

F. If under 18, does not meet the criteria for Avoidant Disorder of Childhood or Adolescence.

301.60 Dependent Personality Disorder

Differential diagnosis. Agoraphobia.

Diagnostic criteria

The following are characteristic of the individual's current and long-term functioning, are not limited to episodes of illness, and cause either significant impairment in social or occupational functioning or subjective distress.

A. Passively allows others to assume responsibility for major areas of life because of inability to function independently (e.g., lets spouse decide what kind of job he or she should have).

B. Subordinates own needs to those of person on whom he or she depends in order to avoid any possibility of having to rely on self, e.g., tolerates abusive spouse.

C. Lacks self-confidence, e.g., sees self as helpless, stupid.

301.40 Compulsive Personality Disorder

Differential diagnosis. Obsessive Compulsive Disorder.

Diagnostic criteria.

At least four of the following are characteristic of the individual's current and long-term functioning, are not limited to episodes of illness, and cause either significant impairment in social or occupational functioning or subjective distress:

(1) restricted ability to express warm and tender emotions, e.g., the individual is unduly conventional, serious and formal, and stingy
(2) perfectionism that interferes with the ability to grasp "the big picture," e.g., preoccupation with trivial details, rules, order, organization, schedules, and lists
(3) insistence that others submit to his or her way of doing things and lack of awareness of the feelings elicited by this behavior, e.g., a husband stubbornly insists his wife complete errands for him regardless of her plans
(4) excessive devotion to work and productivity to the exclusion of pleasure and the value of interpersonal relationships
(5) indecisiveness: decision-making is either avoided, postponed, or protracted, perhaps because of an inordinate fear of making a mistake, e.g., the individual cannot get assignments done on time because of ruminating about priorities

301.84 Passive-Aggressive Personality Disorder

Differential diagnosis. Oppositional Disorder, passive-aggressive maneuvers in situations in which assertive behaviors are not possible.

Diagnostic criteria.

The following are characteristic of the individual's

current and long-term functioning, and are not limited to episodes of illness.

A. Resistance to demands for adequate performance in both occupational and social functioning.

B. Resistance expressed indirectly through at least two of the following:

(1) procrastination
(2) dawdling
(3) stubbornness
(4) intentional inefficiency
(5) "forgetfulness"

C. As a consequence of A and B, pervasive and long-standing social and occupational ineffectiveness (including in roles of housewife or student), e.g., intentional inefficiency that has prevented job promotion.

D. Persistence of the behavior pattern even under circumstances in which more self-assertive and effective behavior is possible.

E. Does not meet the criteria for any other Personality Disorder, and if under age 18, does not meet the criteria for Oppositional Disorder.

301.89 Atypical, Mixed or Other Personality Disorder

If an individual qualifies for any of the specific Personality Disorders, that category should be noted even if some features from other categories are present. For example, an individual who fits the description of Compulsive Personality Disorder should be given that diagnosis even if some mild dependent or paranoid features are present.

When an individual qualifies for two Personality Disorders, multiple diagnoses should be made.

Atypical Personality Disorder should be used when the clinician judges that a Personality Disorder is present but there is insufficient information to make a more specific designation.

Mixed Personality Disorder should be used when the individual has a Personality Disorder that involves features from several of the specific Personality Disorders but does not meet the criteria for any one Personality Disorder.

Other Personality Disorder should be used when the clinician judges that a specific Personality Disorder not included in this classification is appropriate, such as Masochistic, Impulsive, or Immature Personality Disorder. In such instances the clinician should record the specific Other Personality Disorder, using the 301.89 code.

V Codes for Conditions Not Attributable to a Mental Disorder That Are a Focus of Attention or Treatment

In some instances one of these conditions will be noted because, after a thorough evaluation, no mental disorder is found. In other instances the scope of the diagnostic evaluation has not been adequate to determine the presence or absence of a mental disorder but there is a need to note the reason for contact with the mental health care system. (With further information, the presence of a mental disorder may become apparent.) Finally, an individual may have a mental disorder, but the focus of attention or treatment is on a condition that is not due to the mental disorder. For example, an individual with Bipolar Disorder may have marital problems that are not directly related to manifestations of the Affective Disorder but are the principal focus of treatment.

V65.20 Malingering

The essential feature is the voluntary production and presentation of false or grossly exaggerated physical or psychological symptoms. The symptoms are produced in pursuit of a goal that is obviously recognizable with an understanding of the individual's circumstances rather than of his or her individual psychology. Examples of such obviously understandable goals include to avoid military conscription or duty, to avoid work, to obtain financial compensation, to evade criminal prosecution, or to obtain drugs.

The differentiation of Malingering from Factitious Disorder depends on the clinician's judgment as to whether the symptom production is in pursuit of a goal that is obviously recognizable and understandable in the circumstances. Malingering is differentiated from Conversion and the other Somatoform Disorders by the voluntary production of symptoms and by the obvious, recognizable goal.

V62.89 Borderline Intellectual Functioning

This category can be used when a focus of attention or treatment is associated with Borderline Intellectual Functioning, i.e., an IQ in the 71-84 range. The differential diagnosis between Borderline Intellectual Functioning and Mental Retardation (an IQ of 70 or below) is especially difficult and important when certain mental disorders coexist, such as Schizophrenia.

V71.01 Adult Antisocial Behavior

This category can be used when a focus of attention or treatment is adult antisocial behavior that is apparently not due to a mental disorder, such as Conduct Disorder, Antisocial Personality Disorder, or a Disorder of Impulse Control. Examples include the behavior of some professional thieves, racketeers, or dealers in illegal substances.

V71.02 Childhood or Adolescent Antisocial Behavior

Same as above. Examples include isolated antisocial acts of children or adolescents (not a pattern of antisocial behavior).

V62.30 Academic Problem

This category can be used when a focus of attention or treatment is an academic problem that is apparently not due to a mental disorder. An example is a pattern of failing grades or of significant underachievement in an individual with adequate intellectual capacity, in the absence of a Specific Developmental Disorder or any other mental disorder to account for the problem.

V62.20 Occupational Problem

This category can be used when a focus of attention or treatment is an occupational problem that is apparently not due to a mental disorder. Examples include job dissatisfaction and uncertainty about career choices.

V62.82 Uncomplicated Bereavement

This category can be used when a focus of attention

or treatment is a normal reaction to the death of a loved one (bereavement).

A full depressive syndrome frequently is a normal reaction to such a loss, with feelings of depression and such associated symptoms as poor appetite, weight loss, and insomnia. However, morbid preoccupation with worthlessness, prolonged and marked functional impairment, and marked psychomotor retardation are uncommon and suggest that the bereavement is complicated by the development of a Major Depression.

In Uncomplicated Bereavement, guilt, if present, is chiefly about things done or not done at the time of the death by the survivor; thoughts of death are usually limited to the individual's thinking that he or she would be better off dead or that he or she should have died with the person who died. The individual with Uncomplicated Bereavement generally regards the feeling of depressed mood as "normal", although he or she may seek professional help for relief of such associated symptoms as insomnia and anorexia.

V15.81 Noncompliance with Medical Treatment

This category can be used when a focus of attention or treatment is noncompliance with medical treatment that is apparently not due to a mental disorder. Examples include failure to follow a prescribed diet because of religious beliefs or to take required medication because of a considered decision that the treatment is worse than the illness. The major differential is with Personality Disorders with prominent paranoid, passive-aggressive, or masochistic features.

V62.89 Phase of Life Problem or Other Life Circumstance Problem

This category can be used when a focus of attention or treatment is a problem associated with a particular developmental phase or some other life circumstance that is apparently not due to a mental disorder. Examples include problems associated with going to school, separating from parental control, starting a new career, marriage, divorce, and retirement.

V61.10 Marital Problem

This category can be used when a focus of attention or treatment is a marital problem that is apparently not due to a mental disorder. An example is marital conflict related to estrangement or divorce.

V61.20 Parent-Child Problem

This category can be used when a focus of attention or treatment is a parent-child problem that is apparently not due to a mental disorder of the individual (parent or child) who is being evaluated. An example is child abuse not attributable to a mental disorder of the parent.

V61.80 Other Specified Family Circumstances

This category can be used when a focus of attention or treatment is a family circumstance that is apparently not due to a mental disorder of the individual being evaluated and is not a Parent-Child or a Marital Problem. Examples are interpersonal difficulties with an aged in-law, or sibling rivalry.

V62.81 Other Interpersonal Problem

This category can be used when a focus of attention or treatment is an interpersonal problem (other than marital or parent-child) that is apparently not due to a mental disorder of the individual who is being evaluated. Examples are difficulties with co-workers, or with romantic partners.

Additional Codes

300.90 Unspecified Mental Disorder (nonpsychotic)

This is a residual category to be used when enough information is available to rule out a psychotic disorder, but further specification is not possible. In some cases, with more information, the diagnosis can be changed to a specific disorder.

V71.09 No Diagnosis or Condition on Axis I

This category should be used to indicate that following an examination, no Axis I diagnosis or condition (including the V code categories) is present. There may or may not be an Axis II diagnosis.

799.90 Diagnosis or Condition Deferred on Axis I

This category should be used to indicate that there is insufficient information to make any diagnostic judgment about an Axis I diagnosis or condition.

V71.09 No Diagnosis on Axis II

This category should be used to indicate that, following an examination, no Axis II diagnosis (i.e., no Personality Disorder or Specific Developmental Disorder) is present. There may or may not be an Axis I diagnosis or condition.

799.90 Diagnosis Deferred on Axis II

This category should be used to indicate that there is insufficient information to make any diagnostic judgment about an Axis II diagnosis.

Appendix A:

Decision Trees For Differential Diagnosis

Appendix A:

Decision Trees For Differential Diagnosis*

The purpose of these decision trees is to aid the clinician in understanding the organization and hierarchical structure of the classification. Each decision tree starts with a set of clinical features. When one of these features is a prominent part of the presenting clinical picture, the clinician can follow the series of questions to rule in or out various diagnostic categories. The questions are only approximations of the actual diagnostic criteria. The decision trees are not meant to replace the specific diagnostic criteria.

* Prepared by Robert L. Spitzer, M.D. and Janet B.W. Williams, M.S.W.

DIFFERENTIAL DIAGNOSIS OF PSYCHOTIC FEATURES

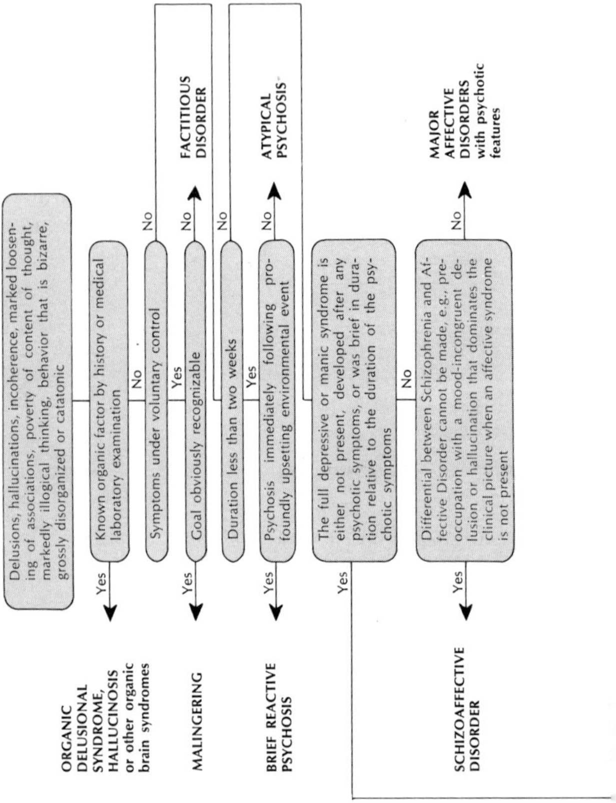

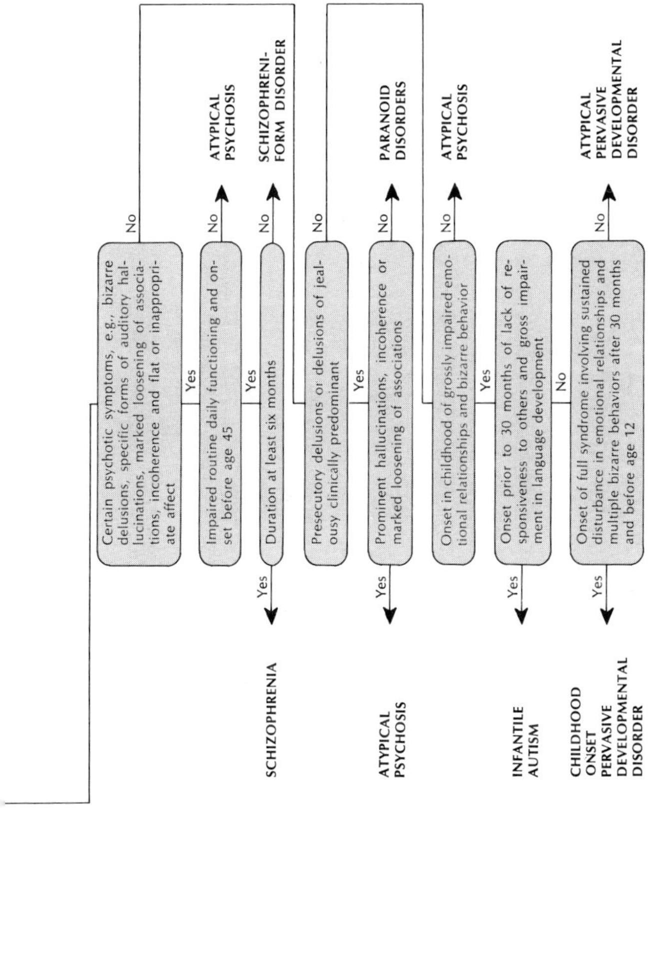
Certain psychotic symptoms, e.g., bizarre delusions, specific forms of auditory hallucinations, marked loosening of associations, incoherence and flat or inappropriate affect
Yes
No
Impaired routine daily functioning and onset before age 45
Yes
No
ATYPICAL PSYCHOSIS
Duration at least six months
Yes
SCHIZOPHRENIA
No
SCHIZOPHRENIFORM DISORDER
Presecutory delusions or delusions of jealousy clinically predominant
Yes
No
Prominent hallucinations, incoherence or marked loosening of associations
Yes
ATYPICAL PSYCHOSIS
No
PARANOID DISORDERS
Onset in childhood of grossly impaired emotional relationships and bizarre behavior
Yes
No
ATYPICAL PSYCHOSIS
Onset prior to 30 months of lack of responsiveness to others and gross impairment in language development
Yes
INFANTILE AUTISM
No
Onset of full syndrome involving sustained disturbance in emotional relationships and multiple bizarre behaviors after 30 months and before age 12
Yes
CHILDHOOD ONSET PERVASIVE DEVELOPMENTAL DISORDER
No
ATYPICAL PERVASIVE DEVELOPMENTAL DISORDER

DIFFERENTIAL DIAGNOSIS OF IRRATIONAL ANXIETY AND AVOIDANCE BEHAVIOR

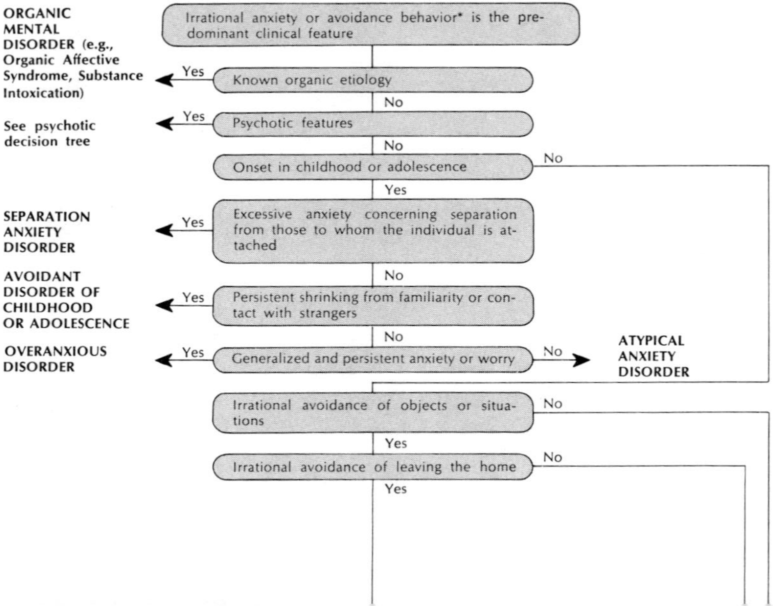

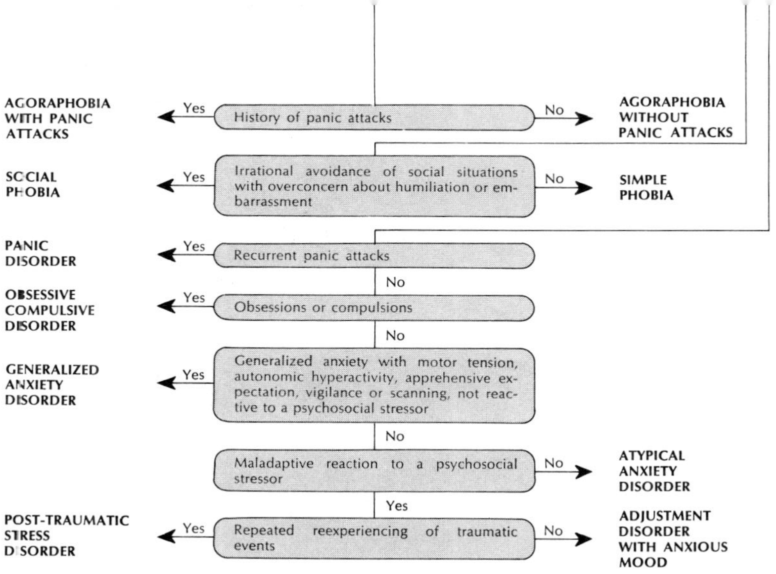

* Also consider Personality Disorders (Axis II), such as Avoidant, Borderline, Compulsive, and Schizotypal Personality Disorders.

DIFFERENTIAL DIAGNOSIS OF MOOD DISTURBANCE

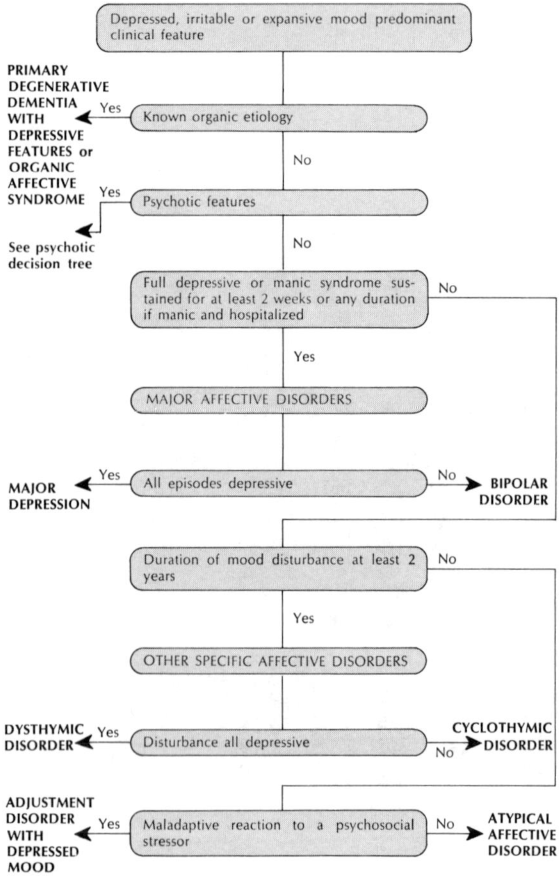

DIFFERENTIAL DIAGNOSIS OF ANTISOCIAL, AGGRESSIVE, DEFIANT, OR OPPOSITIONAL BEHAVIOR

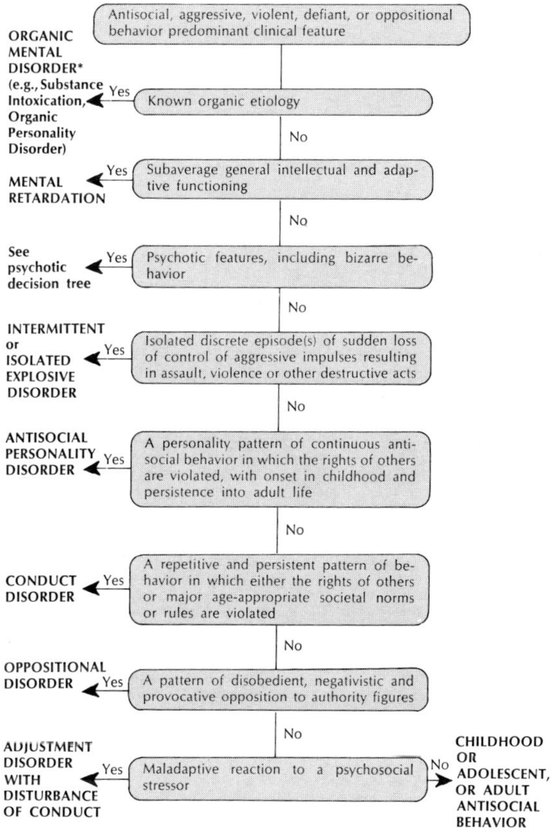
Antisocial, aggressive, violent, defiant, or oppositional behavior predominant clinical feature
ORGANIC MENTAL DISORDER* (e.g., Substance Intoxication, Organic Personality Disorder)
Yes
Known organic etiology
No
MENTAL RETARDATION
Yes
Subaverage general intellectual and adaptive functioning
No
See psychotic decision tree
Yes
Psychotic features, including bizarre behavior
No
INTERMITTENT or ISOLATED EXPLOSIVE DISORDER
Yes
Isolated discrete episode(s) of sudden loss of control of aggressive impulses resulting in assault, violence or other destructive acts
No
ANTISOCIAL PERSONALITY DISORDER
Yes
A personality pattern of continuous antisocial behavior in which the rights of others are violated, with onset in childhood and persistence into adult life
No
CONDUCT DISORDER
Yes
A repetitive and persistent pattern of behavior in which either the rights of others or major age-appropriate societal norms or rules are violated
No
OPPOSITIONAL DISORDER
Yes
A pattern of disobedient, negativistic and provocative opposition to authority figures
No
ADJUSTMENT DISORDER WITH DISTURBANCE OF CONDUCT
Yes
Maladaptive reaction to a psychosocial stressor
No
CHILDHOOD OR ADOLESCENT, OR ADULT ANTISOCIAL BEHAVIOR

* Also consider Intermittent Explosive Disorder which can be diagnosed when symptomatic of an Organic Mental Disorder.

DIFFERENTIAL DIAGNOSIS OF PHYSICAL COMPLAINTS AND IRRATIONAL ANXIETY ABOUT PHYSICAL ILLNESS

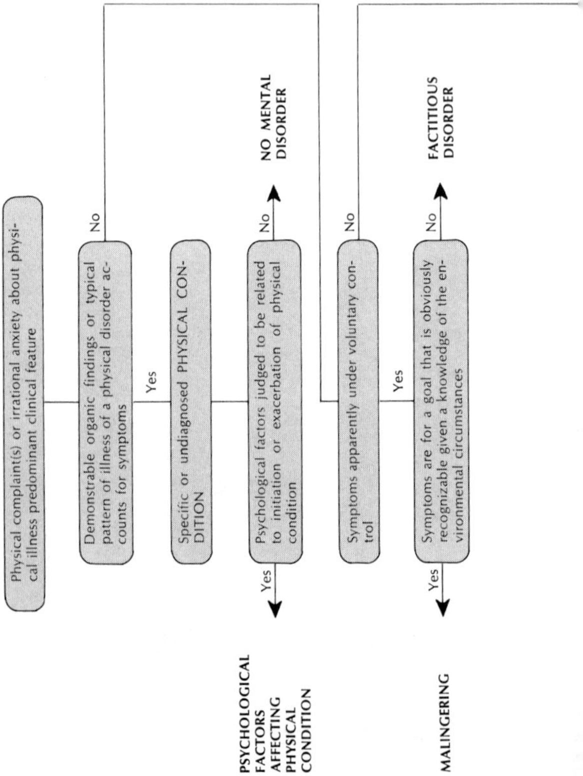

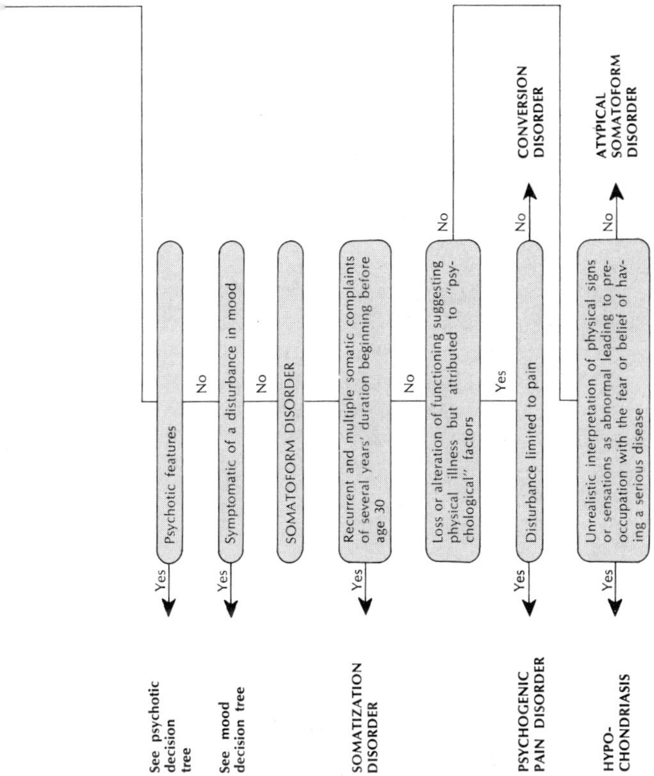

See psychotic decision tree
Yes
Psychotic features
No
See mood decision tree
Yes
Symptomatic of a disturbance in mood
No
SOMATOFORM DISORDER
SOMATIZATION DISORDER
Yes
Recurrent and multiple somatic complaints of several years' duration beginning before age 30
No
Loss or alteration of functioning suggesting physical illness but attributed to "psychological" factors
No
Yes
PSYCHOGENIC PAIN DISORDER
Yes
Disturbance limited to pain
No
CONVERSION DISORDER
HYPO-CHONDRIASIS
Yes
Unrealistic interpretation of physical signs or sensations as abnormal leading to preoccupation with the fear or belief of having a serious disease
No
ATYPICAL SOMATOFORM DISORDER

DIFFERENTIAL DIAGNOSIS OF ACADEMIC OR LEARNING DIFFICULTIES

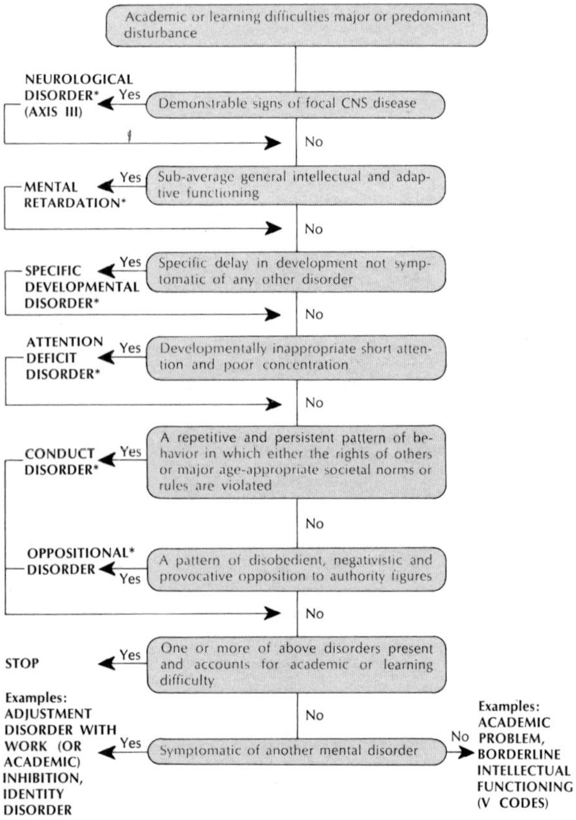
Academic or learning difficulties major or predominant disturbance
NEUROLOGICAL DISORDER* (AXIS III)
Yes
Demonstrable signs of focal CNS disease
No
MENTAL RETARDATION*
Yes
Sub-average general intellectual and adaptive functioning
No
SPECIFIC DEVELOPMENTAL DISORDER*
Yes
Specific delay in development not symptomatic of any other disorder
No
ATTENTION DEFICIT DISORDER*
Yes
Developmentally inappropriate short attention and poor concentration
No
CONDUCT DISORDER*
Yes
A repetitive and persistent pattern of behavior in which either the rights of others or major age-appropriate societal norms or rules are violated
No
OPPOSITIONAL* DISORDER
Yes
A pattern of disobedient, negativistic and provocative opposition to authority figures
No
STOP
Yes
One or more of above disorders present and accounts for academic or learning difficulty
No
Examples: ADJUSTMENT DISORDER WITH WORK (OR ACADEMIC) INHIBITION, IDENTITY DISORDER
Yes
Symptomatic of another mental disorder
No
Examples: ACADEMIC PROBLEM, BORDERLINE INTELLECTUAL FUNCTIONING (V CODES)

* The arrows returning to the trunk of the tree indicate the possibility of multiple diagnoses.

DIFFERENTIAL DIAGNOSIS OF ORGANIC BRAIN SYNDROMES

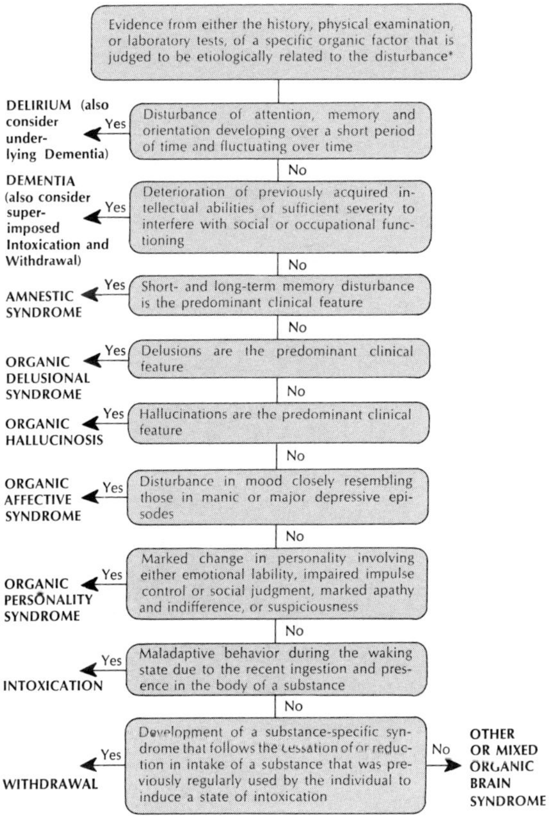

Evidence from either the history, physical examination, or laboratory tests, of a specific organic factor that is judged to be etiologically related to the disturbance*
Disturbance of attention, memory and orientation developing over a short period of time and fluctuating over time
Yes
DELIRIUM (also consider underlying Dementia)
No
Deterioration of previously acquired intellectual abilities of sufficient severity to interfere with social or occupational functioning
Yes
DEMENTIA (also consider superimposed Intoxication and Withdrawal)
No
Short- and long-term memory disturbance is the predominant clinical feature
Yes
AMNESTIC SYNDROME
No
Delusions are the predominant clinical feature
Yes
ORGANIC DELUSIONAL SYNDROME
No
Hallucinations are the predominant clinical feature
Yes
ORGANIC HALLUCINOSIS
No
Disturbance in mood closely resembling those in manic or major depressive episodes
Yes
ORGANIC AFFECTIVE SYNDROME
No
Marked change in personality involving either emotional lability, impaired impulse control or social judgment, marked apathy and indifference, or suspiciousness
Yes
ORGANIC PERSONALITY SYNDROME
No
Maladaptive behavior during the waking state due to the recent ingestion and presence in the body of a substance
Yes
INTOXICATION
No
Development of a substance-specific syndrome that follows the cessation of or reduction in intake of a substance that was previously regularly used by the individual to induce a state of intoxication
Yes
WITHDRAWAL
No
OTHER OR MIXED ORGANIC BRAIN SYNDROME

* In the absence of such evidence, an organic factor can be presumed if conditions outside of the Organic Mental Disorders category have been reasonably excluded and if the disturbance meets the symptomatic criteria for Dementia.

Appendix B:

ICD-9 Classification of Mental Disorders

Appendix B:

ICD-9 Classification of Mental Disorders

ICD-9 Classification of Mental Disorders (without inclusion and exclusion terms) from **Manual of the International Statistical Classification of Diseases, Injuries, and Causes of Death,** Volume 1, World Health Organization, Geneva, 1977

Italics indicate ICD-9 codes and their categories not included in DSM-III that are acceptable to most record keeping systems.

ORGANIC PSYCHOTIC CONDITIONS

Senile and pre-senile organic psychotic conditions

290.0 Senile dementia, simple type
290.1 Pre-senile dementia
290.2 Senile dementia, depressed or paranoid type
290.3 Senile dementia with acute confusional state
290.4 Arteriosclerotic dementia
290.8 Other
290.9 Unspecified

Alcoholic psychoses

291.0 Delirium tremens
291.1 Korsakov's psychosis, alcoholic
291.2 Other alcoholic dementia
291.3 Other alcoholic hallucinosis
291.4 Pathological drunkenness
291.5 Alcoholic jealousy
291.8 Other
291.9 Unspecified

Drug psychoses

292.0 Drug withdrawal syndrome
292.1 Paranoid and/or hallucinatory states induced by drugs
292.2 Pathological drug intoxication
292.8 Other
292.9 Unspecified

Transient organic psychotic conditions

293.0 Acute confusional state
293.1 Subacute confusional state
293.8 Other
393.9 Unspecified

Other organic psychotic conditions (chronic)

294.0 Korsakov's psychosis (non-alcoholic)
294.1 Dementia in conditions classified elsewhere
294.8 Other
294.9 Unspecified

OTHER PSYCHOSES
Schizophrenic psychoses

295.0 Simple type
295.1 Hebephrenic type
295.2 Catatonic type
295.3 Paranoid type
295.4 Acute schizophrenic episode
295.5 Latent schizophrenia
295.6 Residual schizophrenia
295.7 Schizo-affective type
295.8 Other
295.9 Unspecified

Affective psychoses

296.0 Manic-depressive psychosis, manic type
296.1 Manic-depressive psychosis, depressed type
296.2 Manic depressive psychosis, circular type but currently manic
296.3 Manic-depressive psychosis, circular type but currently depressed
296.4 Manic-depressive psychosis, circular type, mixed
296.5 Manic-depressive psychosis, circular type, current condition not specified
296.6 Manic-depressive psychosis, other and unspecified
296.8 Other
296.9 Unspecified

Paranoid states

297.0 Paranoid state, simple

297.1 Paranoia
297.2 Paraphrenia
297.3 Induced psychosis
297.8 Other
297.9 Unspecified

Other non-organic psychoses

298.0 Depressive type
298.1 Excitative type
298.2 Reactive confusion
298.3 Acute paranoid reaction
298.4 Psychogenic paranoid psychosis
298.8 Other and unspecified reactive psychosis
298.9 Unspecified psychosis

Psychoses with origin specific to childhood

299.0 Infantile autism
299.1 Disintegrative psychosis
299.8 Other
299.9 Unspecified

NEUROTIC DISORDERS, PERSONALITY DISORDERS AND OTHER NONPSYCHOTIC MENTAL DISORDERS

Neurotic disorders

300.0 Anxiety states
300.1 Hysteria
300.2 Phobic state
300.3 Obsessive-compulsive disorder
300.4 Neurotic depression
300.5 Neurasthenia
300.6 Depersonalization syndrome
300.7 Hypochondriasis
300.8 Other
300.9 Unspecified

Personality disorders

301.0 Paranoid
301.1 Affective
301.2 Schizoid
301.3 Explosive
301.4 Anankastic

301.5 Hysterical
301.6 Asthenic
301.7 With predominantly sociopathic or asocial manifestations
301.8 Other
301.9 Unspecified

Sexual deviations and disorders

302.0 Homosexuality
302.1 Bestiality
302.2 Paedophilia
302.3 Transvestism
302.4 Exhibitionism
302.5 Trans-sexualism
302.6 Disorders of psychosexual identity
302.7 Frigidity and impotence
302.8 Other
302.9 Unspecified

303. Alcohol dependence

Drug dependence

304.0 Morphine type
304.1 Barbiturate type
304.2 Cocaine
301.3 Cannabis
303.4 Amphetamine type and other psycho-stimulants
304.5 Hallucinogens
304.6 Other
304.7 Combinations of morphine type drug with any other
304.8 Combinations excluding morphine type drug
304.9 Unspecified

Non-dependent abuse of drugs

305.0 Alcohol
305.1 Tobacco
305.2 Cannabis
305.3 Hallucinogens
305.4 Barbiturates and tranquilizers
305.5 Morphine type
305.6 Cocaine type

305.7 Amphetamine type
305.8 Antidepressants
305.9 Other, mixed or unspecified

Physical conditions arising from mental factors

306.0 Musculoskeletal
306.1 Respiratory
306.2 Cardiovascular
306.3 Skin
306.4 Gastro-intestinal
306.5 Genito-urinary
306.6 Endocrine
306.7 Organs of special sense
306.8 Other
306.9 Unspecified

Special symptoms or syndromes not elsewhere classified

307.0 Stammering and stuttering
307.1 Anorexia nervosa
307.2 Tics
307.3 Stereotyped repetitive movements
307.4 Specific disorders of sleep
307.5 Other disorders of eating
307.6 Enuresis
307.7 Encopresis
307.8 Psychalgia
307.9 Other and unspecified

Acute reaction to stress

308.0 Predominant disturbance of emotions
308.1 Predominant disturbance of consciousness
308.2 Predominant psychomotor disturbance
308.3 Other
308.4 Mixed
308.9 Unspecified

Adjustment reaction

309.0 Brief depressive reaction
309.1 Prolonged depressive reaction
309.2 With predominant disturbance of other emotions
309.3 With predominant disturbance of conduct

309.4 With mixed disturbance of emotions and conduct
309.8 Other
309.9 Unspecified

Specific non-psychotic mental disorders following organic brain damage

310.0 Frontal lobe syndrome
310.1 Cognitive or personality change of other type
310.2 Post-concussional syndrome
310.8 Other
310.9 Unspecified
311. Depressive disorder, not elsewhere classified

Disturbance of conduct not elsewhere classified

312.0 Unsocialized disturbance of conduct
312.1 Socialized disturbance of conduct
312.2 Compulsive conduct disorder
312.3 Mixed disturbance of conduct and emotions
312.8 Other
312.9 Unspecified

Disturbance of emotions specific to childhood and adolescence

313.0 With anxiety and fearfulness
313.1 With misery and unhappiness
313.2 With sensitivity, shyness and social withdrawal
313.3 Relationship problems
313.8 Other or mixed
313.9 Unspecified

Hyperkinetic syndrome of childhood

314.0 Simple disturbance of activity and attention
314.1 Hyperkinesis with developmental delay
314.2 Hyperkinetic conduct disorder
313.8 Other
314.9 Unspecified

Specific delays in development

315.0 Specific reading retardation
315.1 Specific arithmetical retardation
315.2 Other specific learning difficulties
315.3 Developmental speech or language disorder
315.4 Specific motor retardation
315.5 Mixed development disorder
315.8 Other
315.9 Unspecified

316. Psychic factors associated with diseases classified elsewhere

317. Mild mental retardation

Other specified mental retardation

318.0 Moderate mental retardation
318.1 Severe mental retardation
318.2 Profound mental retardation

319. Unspecified mental retardation

Appendix C:

Numerical List of Disorders

Appendix C:

Numerical List of Disorders*

290.xx Primary degenerative dementia
290.00 Primary degenerative dementia, senile onset, uncomplicated
290.1x Primary degenerative dementia, presenile onset
290.10 Primary degenerative dementia, presenile onset, uncomplicated
290.11 Primary degenerative dementia, presenile onset, with delirium
290.12 Primary degenerative dementia, presenile onset, with delusions
290.13 Primary degenerative dementia, presenile onset, with depression
290.20 Primary degenerative dementia, senile onset, with delusions
290.21 Primary degenerative dementia, senile onset, with depression
290.30 Primary degenerative dementia, senile onset, with delirium
290.4x Multi-infarct dementia
290.40 Multi-infarct dementia, uncomplicated
290.41 Multi-infarct dementia, with delirium
290.42 Multi-infarct dementia, with delusions
290.43 Multi-infarct dementia, with depression
291.00 Alcohol withdrawal delirium
291.10 Alcohol amnestic disorder
291.2x Dementia associated with alcoholism
291.20 Dementia associated with alcoholism, unspecified
291.21 Dementia associated with alcoholism, mild

* Numbers in parentheses correspond to ICD-9 codes.

291.22 Dementia associated with alcoholism, moderate
291.23 Dementia associated with alcoholism, severe
291.30 Alcohol hallucinosis
291.40 Alcohol idiosyncratic intoxication
291.80 Alcohol withdrawal
292.00 Opioid withdrawal (327.11)
Barbiturate or similarly acting sedative or hypnotic withdrawal (327.01)
Tobacco withdrawal (327.71)
Other or unspecified substance withdrawal (327.91)
Amphetamine or similarly acting sympathomimetic withdrawal (327.31)
Barbiturate or similarly acting sedative or hypnotic withdrawal delirium (327.02)
292.11 Other or unspecified substance delusional disorder (327.95)
Cannabis delusional disorder (327.65)
Hallucinogen delusional disorder (327.55)
Amphetamine or similarly acting sympathomimetic delusional disorder (327.35)
292.12 Other or unspecified substance hallucinosis (327.96)
292.81 Other or unspecified substance delirium (327.92)
Phencyclidine (PCP) or similarly acting arylcyclohexylamine delirium (327.42)
Amphetamine or similarly acting sympathomimetic delirium (327.32)
292.82 Other or unspecified substance dementia (327.93)
292.83 Other or unspecified substance amnestic disorder (327.94)
Barbiturate or similarly acting sedative or hypnotic amnestic disorder (327.04)
292.84 Other or unspecified substance affective disorder (327.97)
Hallucinogen affective disorder (327.57)
292.89 Other or unspecified substance personality disorder (327.98)
292.90 Other or unspecified substance atypical or mixed organic mental disorder (327.99)
Phencyclidine (PCP) or similarly acting aryl-

	cyclohexylamine mixed organic mental disorder (327.49)
293.00	Delirium
293.81	Organic delusional syndrome
293.82	Organic hallucinosis
293.83	Organic affective syndrome
294.00	Amnestic syndrome
294.10	Dementia
294.80	Atypical or mixed organic brain syndrome
295.xx	Schizophrenia with superimposed atypical affective disorder
295.1x	Schizophrenia, disorganized
295.2x	Schizophrenia, catatonic
295.3x	Schizophrenia, paranoid
295.40	Schizophreniform disorder
295.6x	Schizophrenia, residual type
295.70	Schizoaffective disorder
295.9x	Schizophrenia, undifferentiated type
296.2x	Major depression, single episode
296.22	Major depression, single episode, without melancholia
296.23	Major depression, single episode, with melancholia
296.24	Major depression, single episode, with psychotic features
296.3x	Major depression, recurrent
296.32	Major depression, recurrent, without melancholia
296.4x	Bipolar disorder, manic
296.5x	Bipolar disorder, depressed
296.6x	Bipolar disorder, mixed
296.70	Atypical bipolar disorder
296.82	Atypical depression
297.10	Paranoia
297.30	Shared paranoid disorder
297.90	Atypical paranoid disorder
298.30	Acute paranoid disorder
298.80	Brief reactive psychosis
298.90	Atypical psychosis
299.0x	Infantile autism
299.00	Infantile autism, full syndrome present
299.01	Infantile autism, residual state
299.8x	Atypical pervasive developmental disorder
299.9x	Childhood onset pervasive developmental disorder

299.90	Childhood onset pervasive developmental disorder, full syndrome present
299.91	Childhood onset pervasive developmental disorder, residual state
300.00	Atypical anxiety disorder
300.01	Panic disorder
300.02	Generalized anxiety disorder
300.11	Conversion disorder (or hysterical neurosis, conversion type)
300.12	Psychogenic amnesia
300.13	Psychogenic fugue
300.14	Multiple personality
300.15	Atypical dissociative disorder
300.16	Factitious disorder with psychological symptoms
300.19	Atypical factitious disorder with physical symptoms
300.21	Agoraphobia with panic attacks
300.22	Agoraphobia without panic attacks
300.23	Social phobia
300.29	Simple phobia
300.30	Obsessive compulsive disorder (or obsessive compulsive neurosis)
300.40	Dysthymic disorder (or depressive neurosis)
300.60	Depersonalization disorder (or depersonalization neurosis)
300.70	Hypochondriasis (or hypochondriacal neurosis)
	Atypical somatoform disorder
300.81	Somatization disorder
300.90	Unspecified mental disorder (non-psychotic)
301.00	Paranoid personality disorder, coded on Axis II
301.13	Cyclothymic disorder
301.20	Schizoid personality disorder, coded on Axis II
301.22	Schizotypal personality disorder, coded on Axis II
301.40	Compulsive personality disorder, coded on Axis II
301.50	Histrionic personality disorder, coded on Axis II
301.51	Chronic factitious disorder with physical symptoms

301.60	Dependent personality disorder, coded on Axis II
301.70	Antisocial personality disorder, coded on Axis II
301.81	Narcissistic personality disorder, coded on Axis II
301.82	Avoidant personality disorder, coded on Axis II
301.83	Borderline personality disorder, coded on Axis II
301.84	Passive-aggressive personality disorder, coded on Axis II
301.89	Atypical, mixed or other personality disorder, coded on Axis II
302.00	Ego-dystonic homosexuality
302.10	Zoophilia
302.20	Pedophilia
302.30	Transvestism
302.40	Exhibitionism
302.5x	Transsexualism
302.60	Gender identity disorder of childhood
302.70	Atypical psychosexual dysfunction
302.71	Inhibited sexual desire
302.72	Inhibited sexual excitement
302.73	Inhibited female orgasm
302.74	Inhibited male orgasm
302.75	Premature ejaculation
302.76	Functional dyspareunia
302.81	Fetishism
302.82	Voyeurism
302.83	Sexual masochism
302.84	Sexual sadism
302.85	Atypical gender identity disorder
302.89	Psychosexual disorder not elsewhere classified
302.90	Atypical paraphilia
303.00	Alcohol intoxication
303.9x	Alcohol dependence
304.0x	Opioid dependence
304.1x	Barbiturate or similarly acting sedative or hypnotic dependence
304.3x	Cannabis dependence
304.4x	Amphetamine or similarly acting sympathomimetic dependence
304.6x	Other specified substance dependence

304.7x	Dependence on a combination of opioid and other nonalcoholic substances
304.8x	Dependence on a combination of substances, excluding opioids and alcohol
304.9x	Unspecified substance dependence
305.0x	Alcohol abuse
305.01	Alcohol abuse, continuous
305.02	Alcohol abuse, episodic
305.1x	Tobacco dependence
305.2x	Cannabis abuse
305.20	Cannabis intoxication
305.3x	Hallucinogen abuse
305.30	Hallucinogen hallucinosis (327.56)
305.4x	Barbiturate or similarly acting sedative or hypnotic abuse
305.40	Barbiturate or similarly acting sedative or hypnotic intoxication (327.00)
305.5x	Opioid abuse
305.50	Opioid intoxication (327.10)
305.6x	Cocaine abuse
305.60	Cocaine intoxication (327.20)
305.7x	Amphetamine or similarly acting sympathomimetic abuse
305.70	Amphetamine or similarly acting sympathomimetic intoxication (327.30)
305.9x	Other, mixed or unspecified substance abuse
	Phencyclidine (PCP) or similarly acting arylcyclohexylamine abuse (328.4x)
305.90	Phencyclidine (PCP) or similarly acting arylcyclohexylamine intoxication (327.40)
	See specific other PCP disorders
	Caffeine intoxication (327.80)
	Other or unspecified substance intoxication (327.90)
306.51	Functional vaginismus
307.00	Stuttering
307.10	Anorexia nervosa
307.20	Atypical tic disorder
307.21	Transient tic disorder
307.22	Chronic motor tic disorder
307.23	Tourette's disorder
307.30	Atypical stereotyped movement disorder
307.46	Sleep terror disorder (307.49)
307.46	Sleepwalking disorder
307.50	Atypical eating disorder

307.51	Bulimia
307.52	Pica
307.53	Rumination disorder of infancy
307.60	Functional enuresis
307.70	Functional encopresis
307.80	Psychogenic pain disorder
308.30	Post-traumatic stress disorder, acute
309.00	Adjustment disorder with depressed mood
309.21	Separation anxiety disorder (anxiety disorder of childhood or adolescence)
309.23	Adjustment disorder with work (or academic) inhibition
309.24	Adjustment disorder with anxious mood
309.28	Adjustment disorder with mixed emotional features
309.30	Adjustment disorder with disturbance of conduct
309.40	Adjustment disorder with mixed disturbance of emotions and conduct
309.81	Post-traumatic stress disorder, chronic or delayed
309.83	Adjustment disorder with withdrawal
309.90	Adjustment disorder with atypical features
310.10	Organic personality syndrome
312.00	Conduct disorder, undersocialized aggressive
312.10	Conduct disorder, undersocialized nonaggressive
312.21	Conduct disorder, socialized nonaggressive
312.23	Conduct disorder, socialized aggressive
312.31	Pathological gambling
312.32	Kleptomania
312.33	Pyromania
312.34	Intermittent explosive disorder
312.35	Isolated explosive disorder
312.39	Atypical impulse control disorder
312.90	Atypical conduct disorder
313.00	Overanxious disorder (anxiety disorder of childhood or adolescence)
313.21	Avoidant disorder of childhood or adolescence
313.22	Schizoid disorder of childhood or adolescence
313.23	Elective mutism of infancy, childhood or adolescence

313.81	Oppositional disorder of infancy, childhood, or adolescence
313.82	Identity disorder of infancy, childhood, or adolescence
313.89	Reactive attachment disorder of infancy
314.00	Attention deficit disorder without hyperactivity
314.01	Attention deficit disorder with hyperactivity
314.80	Attention deficit disorder, residual type
315.00	Developmental reading disorder (Axis II)
315.10	Developmental arithmetic disorder (Axis II)
315.31	Developmental language disorder (Axis II)
315.39	Developmental articulation disorder (Axis II)
315.50	Mixed specific developmental disorder (Axis II)
315.90	Atypical specific developmental disorder (Axis II)
316.00	Psychological factors affecting physical condition, specify physical condition on Axis III
317.0x	Mild mental retardation
318.0x	Moderate mental retardation
318.1x	Severe mental retardation
318.2x	Profound mental retardation
319.0x	Unspecified mental retardation
319.00	Mental retardation, unspecified without other behavioral symptoms
319.01	Mental retardation, unspecified, with other behavioral symptoms (requiring attention or treatment and that are not part of another disorder)
799.90	Diagnosis or condition deferred on Axis I
799.90	Diagnosis deferred on Axis II

V CODES

V15.81	Noncompliance with medical treatment not attributable to a mental disorder
V61.10	Marital problem not attributable to a mental disorder
V61.20	Parent-child problem not attributable to a mental disorder
V61.80	Other specified family circumstances not attributable to a mental disorder
V62.20	Occupational problem not attributable to a mental disorder

V62.30 Academic problem not attributable to a mental disorder
V62.81 Other interpersonal problem not attributable to a mental disorder
V62.82 Uncomplicated bereavement not attributable to a mental disorder
V62.89 Borderline intellectual functioning not attributable to a mental disorder
V62.89 Phase of life problem or other life circumstance problem not attributable to a mental disorder
V65.20 Malingering not attributable to a mental disorder
V71.01 Adult antisocial behavior not attributable to a mental disorder
V71.02 Childhood or adolescent antisocial behavior not attributable to a mental disorder
V71.09 No diagnosis or condition on Axis I
V71.09 No diagnosis on Axis II

Appendix D:

Alphabetical List of Disorders

Appendix D:

Alphabetical List of Disorders

Abuse, alcohol 305.0x
Abuse, amphetamine or similarly acting sympathomimetic 305.7x
Abuse, barbiturate or similarly acting sedative or hypnotic 305.4x
Abuse, cannabis 305.2x
Abuse, cocaine 305.6x
Abuse, hallucinogen 305.3x
Abuse, opioid 305.5x
Abuse, other, mixed, or unspecified substance 305.9x
Abuse, phencyclidine (PCP) or similarly acting arylcyclohexylamine 305.9x
Academic problem not attributable to a mental disorder V62.30
Acute paranoid disorder 298.30
Acute post-traumatic stress disorder 308.30
Adjustment disorder with anxious mood 309.24
Adjustment disorder with atypical features 309.90
Adjustment disorder with depressed mood 309.00
Adjustment disorder with disturbance of conduct 309.30
Adjustment disorder with mixed disturbance of emotions and conduct 309.40
Adjustment disorder with mixed emotional features 309.28
Adjustment disorder with withdrawal 309.83
Adjustment disorder with work (or academic) inhibition 309.23
Adolescence identity disorder 313.82
Adult antisocial behavior not attributable to a mental disorder V71.01

Affective disorder, hallucinogen 292.84
Affective disorder, other or unspecified substance 292.84
Agoraphobia with panic attacks 300.21
Agoraphobia without panic attacks 300.22
Alcohol abuse 305.0x
Alcohol amnestic disorder 291.10
Alcohol dependence 303.9x
Alcohol hallucinosis 291.30
Alcohol idiosyncratic intoxication 291.40
Alcohol intoxication 303.00
Alcohol withdrawal 291.80
Alcohol withdrawal delirium 291.00
Alcoholism, dementia associated with 291.2x
Alcoholism, dementia associated with, mild 291.21
Alcoholism, dementia associated with, moderate 291.22
Alcoholism, dementia associated with, severe 291.23
Alcoholism, dementia associated with, unspecified 291.20
Amnesia, psychogenic 300.12
Amnestic disorder, alcohol 291.10
Amnestic disorder, barbiturate or similarly acting sedative or hypnotic 292.83
Amnestic disorder, other or unspecified substance 292.83
Amnestic syndrome 294.00
Amphetamine or similarly acting sympathomimetic abuse 305.7x
Amphetamine or similarly acting sympathomimetic delirium 292.81
Amphetamine or similarly acting sympathomimetic delusional disorder 292.11
Amphetamine or similarly acting sympathomimetic dependence 304.4x
Amphetamine or similarly acting sympathomimetic intoxication 305.70
Amphetamine or similarly acting sympathomimetic withdrawal 292.00
Anorexia nervosa 307.10
Antisocial behavior, adult, not attributable to a mental disorder V71.01
Antisocial behavior, childhood or adolescence, not attributable to a mental disorder V71.02
Antisocial personality disorder 301.70

Anxiety disorder, atypical 300.00
Anxiety disorder, generalized 300.02
Arithmetic disorder, developmental 315.10
Articulation disorder, developmental 315.39
Attention deficit disorder, residual type 314.80
Attention deficit disorder with hyperactivity 314.01
Attention deficit disorder without hyperactivity 314.00
Atypical anxiety disorder 300.00
Atypical bipolar disorder 296.70
Atypical conduct disorder 312.90
Atypical depression 296.82
Atypical dissociative disorder 300.15
Atypical eating disorder 307.50
Atypical factitious disorder with physical symptoms 300.19
Atypical gender identity disorder 302.85
Atypical impulse control disorder 312.39
Atypical, mixed or other personality disorder 301.89
Atypical or mixed organic brain syndrome 294.80
Atypical or mixed, other or unspecified substance organic mental disorder 292.90
Atypical paranoid disorder 297.90
Atypical paraphilia 302.90
Atypical pervasive developmental disorder 299.8x
Atypical psychosexual dysfunction 302.70
Atypical psychosis 298.90
Atypical somatoform disorder 300.70
Atypical specific developmental disorder 315.90
Atypical stereotyped movement disorder 307.30
Atypical tic disorder 307.20
Autism, infantile 299.0x
Autism, infantile, full syndrome present 299.00
Autism, infantile, residual state 299.01
Avoidant personality disorder 301.82
Avoidant disorder of childhood or adolescence 313.21

Barbiturate or similarly acting sedative or hypnotic abuse 305.4x
Barbiturate or similarly acting sedative or hypnotic amnestic disorder 292.83
Barbiturate or similarly acting sedative or hypnotic dependence 304.1x

Barbiturate or similarly acting sedative or hypnotic intoxication 305.40
Barbiturate or similarly acting sedative or hypnotic withdrawal 292.00
Barbiturate or similarly acting sedative or hypnotic withdrawal delirium 292.00
Bereavement, uncomplicated, not attributable to a mental disorder V62.82
Bipolar disorder, atypical 296.70
Bipolar disorder, depressed 296.5x
Bipolar disorder, manic 296.4x
Bipolar disorder, mixed 296.6x
Borderline intellectual functioning not attributable to a mental disorder V62.89
Borderline personality disorder 301.83
Brief reactive psychosis 298.80
Bulimia 307.51

Caffeine intoxication 305.90
Cannabis abuse 305.2x
Cannabis delusional disorder 212.11
Cannabis dependence 304.3x
Cannabis intoxication 305.20
Catatonic type schizophrenic disorder 295.2x
Child-parent problem not attributable to a mental disorder V61.20
Childhood gender identity disorder 302.60
Childhood onset pervasive developmental disorder 299.9x
Childhood onset pervasive developmental disorder, full syndrome present 299.90
Childhood onset pervasive developmental disorder, residual state 299.91
Childhood or adolescence avoidant disorder 313.21
Childhood or adolescence oppositional disorder 313.81
Childhood or adolescence overanxious disorder 313.00
Childhood or adolescence schizoid disorder 313.22
Childhood or adolescence separation anxiety disorder 309.21
Childhood or adolescent antisocial behavior not attributable to a mental disorder V71.02
Chronic factitious disorder with physical symptoms 301.51

Chronic motor tic disorder 307.22
Chronic or delayed post-traumatic stress disorder 309.81
Cocaine abuse 305.6x
Cocaine intoxication 305.60
Compulsive disorder, obsessive 300.30
Compulsive personality disorder, Axis II 301.40
Conduct disorder, atypical 312.90
Conduct disorder, socialized, aggressive 312.23
Conduct disorder, socialized, nonaggressive 312.21
Conduct disorder, undersocialized, aggressive 312.00
Conduct disorder, undersocialized, nonaggressive 312.10
Conversion disorder or hysterical neurosis, conversion type 300.11
Cyclothymic disorder 301.13

Delirium 293.00
Delirium, alcohol withdrawal 291.00
Delirium, amphetamine or similarly acting sympathomimetic 292.81
Delirium, barbiturate or similarly acting sedative or hypnotic, withdrawal 292.00
Delirium, other or unspecified substance induced 292.81
Delirium, phencyclidine (PCP) or similarly acting arylcyclohexylamine 292.81
Delusional disorder, amphetamine or similarly acting sympathomimetic induced 292.11
Delusional disorder, cannabis induced 292.11
Delusional disorder, hallucinogen induced 292.11
Delusional disorder, other or unspecified substance induced 292.11
Dementia 294.10
Dementia associated with alcoholism 291.2x
Dementia associated with alcoholism, mild 291.21
Dementia associated with alcoholism, moderate 291.22
Dementia associated with alcoholism, severe 291.23
Dementia associated with alcoholism, unspecified 291.20
Dementia, multi-infarct 290.4x
Dementia, multi-infarct, uncomplicated 290.40
Dementia, multi-infarct, with delirium 290.41

Developmental disorder, pervasive, atypical 299.8x
Developmental disorder, mixed specific 315.50
Developmental disorder, pervasive, childhood onset 299.9x
Developmental disorder, pervasive, childhood onset, full syndrome present 299.90
Developmental disorder, pervasive, childhood onset, residual state 299.91
Developmental language disorder 315.31
Developmental reading disorder 315.00
Diagnosis or condition deferred on Axis I 799.90
Diagnosis deferred on Axis II 799.90
Disorganized type, schizophrenia 295.1x
Dissociative disorder, atypical 300.15
Dyspareunia, functional 302.76
Dysthymic disorder 300.40

Eating disorder, atypical 307.50
Ego-dystonic homosexuality 302.00
Ejaculation, premature 302.75
Elective mutism 313.23
Encopresis, functional 307.70
Enuresis, functional 307.60
Exhibitionism 302.40
Explosive disorder, intermittent 312.34
Explosive disorder, isolated 312.35

Factitious disorder, atypical, with physical symptoms 300.19
Factitious disorder, chronic, with physical symptoms 301.51
Factitious disorder with psychological symptoms 300.16
Family circumstances, other specified, not attributable to a mental disorder V61.80
Female orgasm, inhibited 302.73
Fetishism 302.81
Fugue, psychogenic 300.13
Functional dyspareunia 302.76
Functional encopresis 307.70
Functional enuresis 307.60
Functional vaginismus 306.51

Gambling, pathological 312.31
Gender identity disorder, atypical 302.85

Gender identity disorder of childhood 302.60
Generalized anxiety disorder 300.02

Hallucinogen abuse 305.3x
Hallucinogen affective disorder 292.84
Hallucinogen delusional disorder 292.11
Hallucinogen hallucinosis 305.30
Hallucinosis, alcohol 291.30
Hallucinosis, organic 293.82
Hallucinosis, other or unspecified substance induced 292.12
Histrionic personality disorder, Axis II 301.50
Homosexuality, ego-dystonic 302.00
Hypochondriasis, hypochondriacal neurosis 300.70
Hysterical neurosis, conversion type 300.11

Identity disorder, atypical 302.85
Identity disorder of adolescence 313.82
Idiosyncratic intoxication, alcohol 292.40
Impulse control disorder, atypical 312.39
Infancy reactive attachment disorder 313.89
Infancy rumination disorder 307.53
Infantile autism 299.0x
Infantile autism, full syndrome present 299.00
Infantile autism, residual state 299.01
Inhibited female orgasm 302.73
Inhibited male orgasm 302.74
Inhibited sexual desire 302.71
Inhibited sexual excitement 302.72
Intermittent explosive disorder 312.34
Interpersonal problem, other, not attributable to a mental disorder V62.81
Intoxication, alcohol 303.00
Intoxication, amphetamine or similarly acting sympathomimetic 305.70
Intoxication, barbiturate or similarly acting sedative or hypnotic 305.40
Intoxication, caffeine 305.90
Intoxication, cannabis 305.20
Intoxication, cocaine 305.60
Intoxication, opioid 305.50
Intoxication, phencyclidine (PCP) or similarly acting arylcyclohexylamine 305.90
Intoxication, other or unspecified substance 305.90
Isolated explosive disorder 312.35

Kleptomania 312.32

Language disorder, developmental 315.31
Life problem phase, or other life circumstance problem, not attributable to a mental disorder V62.89

Major depression, recurrent 296.3x
Major depression, single episode 296.2x
Male orgasm, inhibited 302.74
Malingering not attributable to a mental disorder V65.20
Manic, bipolar disorder 296.4x
Marital problem not attributable to a mental disorder V61.10
Masochism, sexual 302.83
Mental retardation, mild 317.0x
Mental retardation, moderate 318.0x
Mental retardation, profound 318.2x
Mental retardation, severe 318.1x
Mental retardation, unspecified 319.0x
Mixed organic mental disorder, PCP induced 292.90
Motor tic disorder, chronic 307.22
Multi-infarct dementia 290.4x
Multi-infarct dementia, uncomplicated 290.40
Multi-infarct dementia with delirium 290.41
Multi-infarct dementia with delusions 290.42
Multi-infarct dementia with depression 290.43
Multiple personality 300.14
Mutism, elective 313.23

Narcissistic personality disorder 301.81
No diagnosis on Axis II V71.09
No diagnosis or condition on Axis I V71.09
Noncompliance with medical treatment not attributable to a mental disorder V15.81

Obsessive compulsive disorder or obsessive compulsive neurosis 300.30
Occupational problem not attributable to a mental disorder V62.20
Opioid abuse 305.5x
Opioid and other nonalcoholic substance dependence 304.7x
Opioid dependence 304.0x
Opioid intoxication 305.50

Opioid withdrawal 292.00
Oppositional disorder of childhood and adolescence 313.81
Organic affective syndrome 293.83
Organic brain syndrome, atypical or mixed 294.80
Organic delusional syndrome 293.81
Organic hallucinosis 293.82
Organic mental disorder, atypical or mixed, other or unspecified substance 292.90
Organic mental disorder, mixed, PCP induced 292.90
Organic personality syndrome 310.10
Orgasm, female inhibited 302.73
Orgasm, male inhibited 302.74
Other interpersonal problem not attributable to a mental disorder V62.81
Other, mixed, or unspecified substance abuse 305.9x
Other or unspecified substance affective disorder 292.84
Other or unspecified substance amnestic disorder 292.83
Other or unspecified substance atypical or mixed organic mental disorder 292.90
Other or unspecified substance delirium 292.81
Other or unspecified substance delusional disorder 292.11
Other or unspecified substance dementia 292.82
Other or unspecified substance hallucinosis 292.12
Other or unspecified substance intoxication 305.90
Other or unspecified substance personality disorder 292.89
Other or unspecified substance withdrawal 292.00
Other specified family circumstances not attributable to a mental disorder V61.80
Other specified substance dependence 304.6x
Overanxious disorder 313.00

Panic disorder 300.01
Paranoia 297.10
Paranoid disorder, acute 298.30
Paranoid disorder, atypical 297.90
Paranoid disorder, shared 297.30
Paranoid personality disorder 301.00
Paranoid type schizophrenic disorder 295.3x
Paraphilia, atypical 302.90

Parent-child problem not attributable to a mental disorder V61.20
Passive-aggressive personality disorder 301.84
Pathological gambling 312.31
Pedophilia 302.20
Personality disorder, antisocial 301.70
Personality disorder, atypical, mixed, or other 301.89
Personality disorder, avoidant 301.82
Personality disorder, borderline 301.83
Personality disorder, compulsive 301.40
Personality disorder, dependent 301.60
Personality disorder, histrionic 301.50
Personality disorder, narcissistic 301.81
Personality disorder, other or unspecified substance induced 292.89
Personality disorder, paranoid 301.00
Personality disorder, passive-aggressive 301.84
Personality disorder, schizoid 301.20
Personality disorder, schizotypal 301.22
Pervasive developmental disorder, atypical 299.8x
Pervasive developmental disorder, childhood onset 299.9x
Pervasive developmental disorder, childhood onset, full syndrome present 299.90
Pervasive developmental disorder, childhood onset, residual state 299.91
Phase of life problem or other life circumstance problem not attributable to a mental disorder V62.89
Phencyclidine (PCP) or similarly acting arylcyclohexlamine abuse 305.9x
Phencyclidine (PCP) or similarly acting arylcyclohexlamine delirium 292.81
Phencyclidine (PCP) or similarly acting arylcyclohexlamine intoxication 305.90
Phencyclidine (PCP) or similarly acting arylcyclohexlamine mixed organic mental disorder 292.90
Phobia, simple 300.29
Phobia, social 300.23
Pica 307.52
Post-traumatic stress disorder, acute 308.30
Post-traumatic stress disorder, atypical anxiety disorder 300.00
Post-traumatic stress disorder, chronic or delayed 309.81
Premature ejaculation 302.75

Primary degenerative dementia 290.xx
Primary degenerative dementia, senile onset 290.1x
Primary degenerative dementia, presenile onset, uncomplicated 290.10
Primary degenerative dementia, presenile onset with delirium 290.11
Primary degenerative dementia, presenile onset with delusions 290.12
Primary degenerative dementia, presenile onset with depression 290.13
Primary degenerative dementia, senile onset, uncomplicated 290.00
Primary degenerative dementia, senile onset with delirium 290.30
Primary degenerative dementia, senile onset with delusions 290.20
Primary degenerative dementia, senile onset with depression 290.21
Profound mental retardation 318.2x
Psychogenic amnesia 300.12
Psychogenic fugue 300.13
Psychogenic pain disorder 307.80
Psychological factors affecting physical condition 316.00
Psychosexual disorder not elsewhere classified 302.89
Psychosexual dysfunction, atypical 302.70
Psychosis, atypical 298.90
Psychosis, brief reactive 298.80
Pyromania 312.33

Reactive attachment disorder of infancy 313.89
Reading disorder, developmental 315.00
Residual type schizophrenic disorder 295.6x
Rumination disorder of infancy 307.53

Sadism, sexual 302.84
Shared paranoid disorder 297.30
Schizoaffective disorder 295.70
Schizoid disorder of childhood or adolescence 313.22
Schizoid personality disorder 301.20
Schizophrenia, catatonic type 295.2x
Schizophrenia, disorganized type 295.1x

Schizophrenia, paranoid type 295.3x
Schizophrenia, residual type 295.6x
Schizophrenia, undifferentiated type 295.9x
Schizophreniform disorder 295.40
Schizotypal personality disorder 301.22
Separation anxiety disorder of childhood or adolescence 309.21
Severe mental retardation 318.1x
Sexual desire, inhibited 302.71
Sexual excitement, inhibited 302.72
Sexual masochism 302.83
Sexual sadism 302.84
Shared paranoid disorder 297.30
Simple phobia 300.29
Sleep terror disorder 307.46
Sleepwalking disorder 307.46
Social phobia 300.23
Socialized aggressive conduct disorder 312.33
Socialized nonaggressive conduct disorder 312.21
Somatization disorder 300.81
Somatoform disorder, atypical 300.70
Stereotyped movement disorder, atypical 307.30
Stress disorder, post-traumatic, acute 308.30
Stress disorder, post-traumatic, chronic or delayed 309.81
Stuttering 307.00
Substance, other, mixed, or unspecified, abuse 305.9x
Substance, other or unspecified, affective disorder 292.84
Substance, other or unspecified, atypical or mixed organic mental disorder 292.90
Substance, other or unspecified, amnestic disorder 292.83
Substance, other or unspecified, delirium 292.81
Substance, other or unspecified, delusional disorder 292.11
Substance, other or unspecified, dementia 292.82
Substance, other or unspecified, hallucinosis 292.12
Substance, other or unspecified, intoxication 305.90
Substance, other or unspecified, personality disorder 292.89
Substance, other or unspecified, withdrawal 292.00
Substance, other specified, dependence 304.6x
Substance, unspecified, dependence 304.9x

Tic disorder, atypical 307.20
Tic disorder, chronic motor 307.22
Tic disorder, transient 307.21
Tobacco dependence 305.1x
Tobacco withdrawal 292.00
Tourette's disorder 307.23
Transient tic disorder 307.21
Transsexualism 302.5x
Transvestism 302.30

Uncomplicated bereavement not attributable to a mental disorder V62.82
Undersocialized aggressive conduct disorder 312.00
Undersocialized nonaggressive conduct disorder 312.10
Undifferentiated type schizophrenia 295.9x
Unspecified mental disorder, nonpsychotic 300.90
Unspecified substance dependence 304.9x

Vaginismus, functional 306.51
Voyeurism 302.82

Withdrawal, alcohol 291.80
Withdrawal, amphetamine or similarly acting sympathomimetic 292.00
Withdrawal, barbiturate or similarly acting sedative or hypnotic 292.00
Withdrawal delirium, alcohol 291.00
Withdrawal delirium, barbiturate or similarly acting sedative or hypnotic 292.00
Withdrawal, opioid 292.00
Withdrawal, other or unspecified substance 292.00
Withdrawal, tobacco 292.00
Work or academic inhibition 309.23

Zoophilia 302.10

Index of Diagnostic Terms

This index includes names of diagnostic categories in DSM-III as well as other widely used diagnostic terms.